p.21 "These computers don't change the quality of care that patients receive
& p.34 - just (only) eliminate paper work

p.21 "The next big thing or "big data" BTOR
using large databases... searching for breakthroughs in the treatment, & prevention or prediction of illness."

p.33 U.S. gov. subsidizes [caregiver] in order that health care providers get into... "best medical practices"

p.10 pre-care principle & drug safety

p.18 — members who volunteer to allow their records to be used for research

p.22 physicians are required to use what they learn in medical school

TRANSFORMING HEALTH CARE

TRANSFORMING HEALTH CARE

The Financial Impact of Technology, Electronic Tools, and Data Mining

PHILIP FASANO

WILEY

John Wiley & Sons, Inc.

Cover image: © Max Delston/IStockPhoto
Cover design: John Wiley & Sons, Inc.

Published by John Wiley & Sons, Inc., Hoboken, New Jersey.
Published simultaneously in Canada.

For general information on our other products and services or for technical support, please contact our Customer Care Department within the United States at (800) 762-2974, outside the United States at (317) 572-3993, or fax (317) 572-4002.

Wiley publishes in a variety of print and electronic formats and by print-on-demand. Some material included with standard print versions of this book may not be included in e-books or in print-on-demand. If this book refers to media such as a CD or DVD that is not included in the version you purchased, you may download this material at http://booksupport.wiley.com. For more information about Wiley products, visit www.wiley.com.

Library of Congress Cataloging-in-Publication Data:

Fasano, Philip.
   Transforming health care : the financial impact of technology, electronic tools, and data mining / Philip Fasano.
      pages cm
   Includes bibliographical references and index.
   ISBN 978-1-118-35000-3 (cloth); ISBN 978-1-118-42034-8 (ebk);
   ISBN 978-1-118-43397-3 (ebk); ISBN 978-1-118-41678-5 (ebk)
     1. Medical technology—Economic aspects. 2. Medical care, Cost of. I. Title.
   R855.3.F37   2013
   610.285—dc23

                                         2012041642

Printed in the United States of America
10 9 8 7 6 5 4 3 2 1

Contents

v

CONTENTS

Contents

CONTENTS

Foreword

Advances in medicine and biomedical sciences have leveraged technology for the entire history of the medical profession. Extensive improvements have been achieved through technologies that have been able to help physicians first understand the human body, and then diagnose and treat patients. Technology has played a dramatic role in helping physicians to observe, and to actually view, the inner workings of the human body in ways that were unimaginable just 100 years ago. From the advent of the first X-ray machine in 1895 to more recent advances in imaging that include MRI machines, CT scans, and PET scans, we have made remarkable strides. In addition, innovation in technology has touched the areas of pharmacotherapy, radiotherapy, immunotherapy, surgical devices, and surgical techniques including the use of robots. The list goes on and continues to grow as new applications of existing technology are developed and new technologies themselves are invented.

But in the care delivery realm—the methods and techniques we have used to process and deliver patient care—technology has only become part of that thinking and work more recently. In this book, Phil Fasano initiates an important conversation about how health care uses patient information, electronic access, tools, and teams to deliver true 21st-century information-age health care. The electronic health record does not come with an owner's manual that tells us how to use it and how to transform care. But as we use it inside an organization like Kaiser Permanente and as part of a global learning community, we put this important technology central in the delivery of care. As many organizations and professionals begin to navigate this journey of how to use the information-age tools to transform health care, Phil provides some important starting thoughts, experiences, and challenges.

Phil joined Kaiser Permanente in 2007, stepping out of the world of finance and into a new world of health care. During his time here, Kaiser Permanente has created better tools and platforms to deliver smarter, more connected care that is also preventive and affordable. His work has significantly contributed to our ability to measure and compare the care we deliver, which lends itself to improving quality and safety. And, it has helped move us toward our goal of real-time, personalized healthcare for our more than 9 million members. The centerpiece of the technology platform is Kaiser Permanente HealthConnect®, the world's largest civilian electronic health record. KP HealthConnect gives the organization's over 16,000 physicians immediate access to patients' status and medical history, as well as support for making decisions using evidence-based practice guidelines and the latest medical research. Kaiser Permanente members can easily make and reschedule appointments, check lab results, and send emails to care providers via My Health Manager, the online personal health record that connects directly with KP HealthConnect.

The deployment of KP HealthConnect symbolizes the realization of a vision for health information technology that began 50 years earlier. That journey includes some fascinating twists and turns. In the end, I believe that Dr. Sidney Garfield, the innovative physician leader and partner to Henry Kaiser who first saw the potential of and then advocated for the use of computers in healthcare delivery, would be proud of what we have achieved. He would also be enthusiastic about the next phase of this journey to contribute to and understand how inventors and entrepreneurial minds will take us to the next phase in analytics and virtual capabilities. The emerging ideas around "big data" and how to effectively use the rapidly increasing amounts of data we can now collect through the digitization of healthcare are critical in thinking about how to deliver care. We need to learn to ask the right questions about the masses of data becoming available—questions that turn that data into information and ultimately knowledge; questions that reflect how best to provide care for patients and improve the health of populations; questions that support patients' abilities to take care of themselves and better understand their health, questions that drive learning and research, and questions that drive collaboration and support across the health care sector.

Phil describes the path Kaiser Permanente has been on, how the industry has changed in recent years, and shares the challenges and opportunities that we have experienced. More importantly, the book lays out the challenges and opportunities that remain before us. It reminds us that we can learn from the progress we have made, particularly when it comes to utilizing the tools and technology that allow physicians to better serve, communicate with, and heal their patients. This increased use of information technology has enabled change as well as helped create an environment where the rate of change has accelerated and the locus of information, business transactions, and "power" has moved to the patient. And despite the temptation to focus on the "bells and whistles" sometimes associated with information technology efforts, Phil makes sure to never lose sight of the fact that the patient is at the center of the effort. In this book, he acknowledges that ultimately, the biggest challenges go beyond software and dollars. It is clear that health information technology has to prove to doctors and patients that it is safe, trustworthy, and better than that familiar manila folder.

As a physician leader, I am always looking for books, case studies, surveys, and data that help me and my colleagues to not only better serve our members, but also help health care improve—globally. In this important book, Phil not only lays out a comprehensive and accessible picture of where we have been and where we are, but also clearly points the way for health information technology to the future.

Jack Cochran, MD
Executive Director, The Permanente Federation,
Kaiser Permanente
December 2012

Preface

In 2007 after a 25-year career in information technology (IT) in the financial services industry, I joined Kaiser Permanente as the organization's chief information officer. It was my first foray into health care. Given my long tenure in banking and on Wall Street, I had to learn a whole new way of looking at technology and its power to transform an industry. The principles are the same, but the stakes are different—higher—and that makes for a unique set of cultural challenges and opportunities.

When I had been at Kaiser Permanente for two years, George Halvorson, the organization's chairman and CEO, suggested I consider writing a book about technology and health care. I had absorbed a lot on the job, but hardly enough to add my voice to the complex discourse on care quality, exploding costs, system dysfunctions, and health-care reform options. You see, I am an ardent believer in what

Outliers author Malcolm Gladwell calls the "10,000 hours" concept. The basic idea is that once you have 10,000 hours of experience in a given realm, you can then be considered an expert in that subject.

I first put pen to paper—or fingertips to keyboard—later that year, about the time I passed the 10,000-hour mark. I typed out thoughts on my laptop and then my iPad in airports, on planes, on weekends. I started with my own observations of the way things were and my developing vision of how they could be if we could clear some obstacles. This process went on for barely a blink of an eye, but by the time we started researching and editing in earnest, the technology and healthcare landscapes had changed so significantly that it was already time to update our thinking. That is one of the exciting parts of health IT. You never stand still. The technology continues to accelerate at a breathtaking pace. The energy behind healthcare innovation, including health IT technology, continues to build and is helping propel us to a new era of health care. In this era, the patient is truly at the center; and well-integrated, conveniently available information is leveraged to improve health, deliver better service to happier patients, and reduce costs across the system.

I may have just passed my 10,000-hour milestone, but I owe a debt of gratitude to the many colleagues who lent me their expertise, taught me, and coached me through all of those hours. You can be sure that their voices, their experience, and their vision are as much a part of this book as my own. Among so many great physicians that I've been privileged to interact with, they include physician leaders Dr. Jack Cochran, Dr. Robert Pearl, Dr. Jeff Weisz, and Dr. John Mattison. They all have generously contributed their years of experience in the most leading-edge medicine and innovative health IT to help me better understand the world of health care. My colleagues in leadership at Kaiser Permanente have inspired me with their passion for every patient, and for a vision of better health in this country. They include Bernard Tyson, Kathy Lancaster, Dr. Jed Weissberg, Charles Columbus, Anthony Barrueta, Mark Zemelman, Dr. Ray Baxter, Dr. Arthur Southam, and Diane Gage-Lofgren. And, of course, George Halvorson, who I have always said is really the CIO of Kaiser Permanente. His vision, mentorship, and partnership are inextricably linked to my own passion for transforming health care through technology.

The real reason I joined Kaiser Permanente was to contribute to an industry where the results of my efforts might have a small part in creating better health for all Americans. I knew that the healthcare system was in desperate need of transformation, and I thought I might be able to transfer my experiences in industry-transforming technology to what I saw as a more worthy cause.

I still feel that way. More than ever, I am encouraged by the advances I see every day: technology in the hands of physicians and caregivers who are relentlessly committed to the health of their patients. We can learn so much from the application of technology across various industries, but I've learned that technology in health care is not exactly the same as technology anywhere else. It comes with a heavy dose of government regulation, of course, but it is also best served with especially generous portions of patient-focus and compassion.

As you read what I hope will be some inspiring predictions and heartening examples of how health information technology is already transforming health care, ask yourself how in your position—whether you are a technologist, a healthcare provider, or another player in the healthcare and technology industries—you can accelerate the change that we know must come to health care.

I've really just barely started on this journey. I've joined the journey of extraordinary physicians, business leaders, and technologists. I know we can do better. Join us on the journey.

Phil Fasano

Acknowledgments

"The discipline of writing something down is the first step toward making it happen."

Lee Iacocca was right about that, but there is a lot of distance between writing a first draft and publishing a book. I could not have gone that distance without a lot of support and assistance from a number of people.

Sari Harrar and Christie Aschwanden turned my drafts, notes, and sometimes random thoughts into well-crafted prose. The readers of this book benefited greatly from their efforts. I work in an organization that values evidence-based medicine and wanted to back up the ideas in this book with compelling evidence. Deborah Soule tracked down scores of clinical studies, statistical reports, business case studies, and newspaper articles to illustrate and support my vision of transformative healthcare IT. Sandy Trupp took care of the very important step of finding a publisher. At Wiley,

I was fortunate to work with Emilie Herman and Debra Englander.

Once that first step toward this book was taken, Amanda Higgins kept me on track for the countless steps that followed. She worked tirelessly to secure resources and contributed her top-notch writing and editing skills when needed. Amanda understands that "words matter" and she helped make sure the words and thoughts expressed in this book will have the opportunity to matter on a large stage. Christina Holmes provided outstanding project management support. Diane Fraser lent her excellent editing skills to get us across the finish line. I owe thanks also to Cameron Terry for his innovative thinking on the future of health IT.

You would think that, after 30 years of marriage, I would know better than to leave my dear and supportive wife Judy at the end of these acknowledgments. But the truth is, she and each of my five children—Philip, Melissa, Jonathan, Jillian, and Matthew—are fundamental to everything I do. Their constant support has enabled me to focus on our mission at Kaiser Permanente and internalize the lessons I've learned in this book.

Introduction

Tyler Lee is excited. His grandmother is arriving from Harrisburg, Pennsylvania for a visit. As soon as the family picks Grandma up at Oakland International Airport, they are off to a family picnic in the park. Tyler can't wait to show her how fast he can run.

Before she left the house that morning, Tyler's grandma clipped on her insulin pump, fully integrated with her smart mirror, to check her glucose level trends for the week. Good news: 108 mg/dl; she's managing her type 1 diabetes well. To the kitchen for a bite to eat before leaving and to pack a snack for the flight. Her refrigerator was expecting her and as she placed her hand on the handle, it flashes a list of suggested snacks to help control her blood sugar.

Meanwhile, in Oakland, her daughter is reading the news and e-mail on her tablet computer. Her husband and Tyler come through with the ice chest and soccer ball. An alert from her healthcare provider pops up on her tablet:

"Heat wave alert. High asthma risk." She double checks her backpack to make sure she has Tyler's inhaler.

At the Oakland Kaiser Permanente Medical Center, nurses are getting ready for their shift. Their computer, as elegant as a piece of art, lets them move from one display to the next with the ease of a hand swipe or a touch on a piece of information to drill down. The computer is using enterprise analytics to scan the environment: How many beds are available? What surgeries are scheduled? What is the status of the ER? What's the weather, the pollen count? Any public health trends? What are the wait time trends, status of the computing networks? They are given a recommendation to schedule an additional care team to cope with the coming heat wave. With a few more waves of the hand, on-call team members get the alert.

Grandma arrives at the airport to Tyler's hugs and her daughter's big smile.

At the park, Tyler and his cousins play soccer while the grown-ups talk. Tyler's wrist device monitors his vital signs (heart rate, respiratory rate, biometrics) and sends updates to Mom's smartphone. He's doing just fine; his risk of asthma attack is very low, despite his energetic soccer performance.

Suddenly, Grandma feels dizzy. Although she insists she's just fine, an uncle uses his Kaiser Permanente mobile app for a virtual triage. The recommendation: get Grandma to the hospital. In the car, the app directs them to the nearest Kaiser Permanente Urgent Care facility. In the backseat, Grandma authorizes her healthcare provider, Geisinger Health System, to share her medical records by simply sending a fingerprint from her daughter's tablet computer.

Now care teams from both providers—Grandma's care team and Kaiser Permanente Urgent Care—are alert and ready to give her the best care possible through health information exchange. By the time she arrives in Urgent Care, a new patient record and protocol are already set up. When the doctor orders an IV pump, a nurse gets the order on her smartphone, which also shows her a map indicating which room Grandma is in. When it comes to inserting the IV needle, the nurse dons augmented reality (AR) glasses that can help her locate the right vein on the first try—clinical technology that means a better experience for the patient.

On the large display screen in her room, Grandma can't help but smile at a message and drawing from Tyler, "Feel better, Grandma," sent from Dad's smartphone.

When the doctor arrives, she initiates a live consultation with Grandma's Geisinger doctor back home. Together, they discuss her recent lab work and ongoing trends. Turns out she was dehydrated from the plane ride and the heat. She will need to watch that.

Daughter and Grandma send out an update on Facebook from their in-room tablet and display that all is well. That feedback is also captured in her patient record.

That night, the family hugs each other a little tighter before bed. It's low tech, but high touch.

This scenario isn't as far-fetched as you might think. It provides a look into what could be the near future, where information technology enables real-time, personalized care resulting in improved wellness and affordability. That includes:

- Electronic health records with clean and intuitive interfaces.
- Mobile tools that incorporate user identification, personalized content and contact channel options, and financial management.
- Mobile wellness and health management tools for diagnosis, wellness, patient-provider communications, live nurse triage, and advice lines and location information.

- Health Information Exchanges—interoperability and care coordination enabled by the Care Connectivity Consortium national health information network.
- Advanced analytics, enterprise-wide and seamlessly integrated into electronic health records and workflow for doctors and nurses.
- Clinical technology integration of biometric devices (monitors, ventilators, pumps, glucometers) in both medical and home settings into core care systems.
- Virtual collaboration tools offering improved communication capabilities (videoconferencing, telemedicine, smart messaging boards).
- Social media convergence to improve service levels.

Much of this technology is in use in some form today, although it is hardly integrated and certainly not this seamlessly. Technology has already transformed countless industries and our everyday lives. It also has fueled astonishing improvements in health care. But we can do more. This book examines the potential for information technology to vastly improve the quality, efficiency, and cost-effectiveness of health care. Here is an overview of what you will be reading about.

Envision a future where health care is seamless and efficient, outcomes are high quality, and your health and the health of the nation are far better. That future rests on exchanging outmoded paper records for electronic health records, or EHRs. This change is already under way and is picking up steam thanks to a federal mandate for the adoption of EHRs no later than 2014. But many healthcare organizations have already moved to the next phase: implementing electronic medical records (EMRs) that integrate information not only from physician office visits, but from other systems such as pharmacies and laboratories. In effect, EMRs take an individual's medical information out of the silos created by stand-alone systems and let those systems talk to and inform each other. Those "conversations" will enable us to achieve the true transformative power of healthcare IT.

The next step will take us beyond the walls of individual healthcare organizations and medical practices. It will enable the exchange of information across organizations and across the country. These health information exchanges (HIEs) will give you and your doctor secure, up-to-date information needed to make the right decisions for your care. But these HIEs can't be created or maintained without financial support. We will have to find a way to monetize them so they are self-sustaining. Drawing from my background in financial services, I believe the Fedwire system offers a model for what are now being called health finance networks.

Of course, all of this will take investment and, as a diehard capitalist, I would not want to go too far in this book before addressing that essential topic. The coming transformation of healthcare IT presents significant opportunities for entrepreneurs and established technology firms, venture and angel capitalists to invest and reap the benefits of their investments. The options for the kinds of technology investments that will be needed are almost limitless. They range from mobile platforms, software, and apps to the software and hardware needed to enable virtual consultations through telehealth technologies.

Although the private, high-tech sector is essential to the future of health care, it will have the support of two other highly engaged partners. One of these change agents is the federal government. Its role is primarily in providing guardrails (mandates), handrails (regulations), and connectors (for example, summit meetings and conferences where interested parties can share successes, challenges, ideas, and questions). The other is healthcare plans and payers. We must, and are, finding the economic advantages to technology-enabled care delivery that puts patient health and convenience above fee-for-service treatments and tests.

How can we be sure this transformation will work? There are no guarantees, but we have examples in other countries. This book presents three case studies from countries with high levels of EHR adoption and well-connected systems. They paint pictures of how we might proceed and what health care will look like when we arrive.

The farther we look into the future, the more exciting the prospects become. Robust EMRs and secure HIEs will gather impressive volumes of data. The healthcare industry will need to learn to use the same sophisticated data-mining techniques now employed by firms in the hospitality, consumer goods, logistics, and financial sectors. This wealth of data, in the hands of skilled, trained health data analysts, may well provide medical breakthroughs every bit as important to our well-being as the discovery of penicillin.

Better preventive care has long been an objective of modern medicine—indeed, that was one of the founding principles of Kaiser Permanente—and I include two examples of how electronic systems allow us to live up to that promise. Better still, the data and technologies at the heart of healthcare IT will enable us to move into the realm of predictive care, giving individuals yet more control over their health and well-being.

Certain threads reappear throughout the book: The imperative for secure systems that respect and protect the privacy and confidentiality of our health information. The criticality of coordinated systems to drive down costs while improving health. The need to understand the business case for healthcare IT. And most of all, the transformative power of technology to make health care easier, more convenient, and more personal for everyone who encounters it.

TRANSFORMING HEALTH CARE

Chapter 1

The Emergence of Electronic Tools

Seventy-three cents won't buy much these days. Most daily newspapers cost at least a dollar. Same for a candy bar or a pack of gum. But 73 cents is the going price for photocopying one page of an individual's medical record.

Regina Holliday learned that from the medical records department at the hospital where her husband Fred had been diagnosed and treated for kidney cancer. Oh, and it would take 21 days for the records to be processed and given to her. Within 24 hours, Fred's new doctors arranged for Regina to collect the records, not as his spouse, but as a courier. Twenty-one days melted into two hours—the time needed to print a copy. Regina read that copy and kept it, sadly aware of the power of immediate access to vital medical information that might have improved Fred's care.

Near the end, Fred spent time in hospice care. There, the litany started all over again. "Fred, we have just a few questions about your medical history," the nurse began, and asked Regina to leave the room. Regina refused, telling the nurse, "You're going to need me." Fred, too sick to reply, asked Regina to show the nurse his records. And she could. She opened her binder and started telling Fred's story.

In the 11 weeks of his treatment, Fred was in five different medical facilities. If Regina had been required to wait 21 days for each set of records to be produced, she would still have been waiting as she prepared for her husband's memorial service.

Today, Regina Holliday is a "patients arts advocate," advocating for electronic health records (EHRs). You can watch her video, produced by the federal Office of the National Coordinator for Health Information Technology, on YouTube.[1]

Her message is simple: "EHRs save lives." She is right.

Real-Time Health Care Begins

The story begins with two medical records—one crammed into a battered manila folder, the other digital.

The paper chart, virtually unchanged in format since the 1950s, looks impressively hefty. Average weight: 1½ pounds. Yet despite its girth, the classic compendium of appointment notes and test results that your doctor riffles through at every office visit is likely missing key data about your health. In one analysis of 1,628 medical records published in the *British Medical Journal*, 40 percent omitted an important diagnosis, 30 percent didn't list the names of drugs pre-scribed, and most left out patients' occupations, marital sta-tus, even their ages.[2] No wonder a frustrated internist wrote several years ago in the *Annals of Internal Medicine* that "med-ical records, which have long been faulty, contain more distorted, deleted, and misleading information than ever before."[3]

But that's not all. Illegible handwriting—found in 16 percent of medical charts in another study[4]—makes matters worse. So does the fact that in doctors' offices and in hos-pitals, up to 30 percent of files can't be found at all when they're needed.[5] This leads to repeated tests, delays in treat-ment, and decisions based on not quite all the facts. In a worst-case scenario, paper records are easily destroyed by fires, floods, earthquakes, and hurricanes. Hurricane Katrina destroyed an estimated 1 million charts in New Orleans;[6] still more survived but were inaccessible to the city's mil-lion-plus displaced residents—harming the health of people with diabetes, cancer, AIDS, and other health conditions who needed care.

The electronic health record? Paperless, your EHR lives in a server in your doctor's office or hospital or on the Internet. It's available with the click of a mouse or a couple of keystrokes. You may be able to access parts of it yourself, from home—and so can your doctor, making after-hours emergencies easier to handle and a quick check of your lat-est lab results more convenient. In a well-connected system, other specialists can read and contribute, making your record more complete (and eliminating the need to drag the whole file with you from doctor to doctor, or wait weeks while a copy is mailed across town).

Digital files aren't perfect, of course—a recent Dutch comparison of 32 pediatricians' records found that doctors were leaving information out of electronic records—a failure attributed to their learning curve using the brand-new system.[7] There will be bumps like that in the road ahead as doctors and their staffs adjust to new forms of data entry (which, by the way, are getting easier every day). But studies show conclusively that digital medical records reduce errors, make health care more efficient, and—most important of all—improve health and save lives. And when the data's stored online (a development in health IT we'll return to later in this chapter), it's safe from physical harm and accessible from anyplace.

Despite the clear advantages, which type of record do most Americans have? Paper.

The Paperless Revolution: Let's Get Going!

Before describing why the move away from paper files is essential and how it is happening, I want to define the basic building blocks of a digital record-keeping system. It starts with an electronic medical record, or EMR. In effect, EMRs are digital versions of the manila folders found in file drawers in doctors' offices. They contain the medical history of all the patients seen in a given medical practice. Although EMRs are an improvement over paper records—they allow doctors to track a patient's progress and flag the need for preventive or follow-up care, for example—their usefulness is limited to the practice that created and uses them.[8]

Electronic health records, or EHRs, capture far more information from more sources. An EHR goes outside of the physician's office to include laboratory test results, pharmacy records, and notes from specialists or others involved in a patient's care. Most importantly, EHR data "can be created, managed, and consulted by authorized clinicians and staff across more than one healthcare organization." The information in an EHR follows you throughout your encounters with the healthcare system, whether those happen in your doctor's office or the hospital, in the town where you grew up or in your new home across the country.[9]

How far along are we in adopting EMRs and EHRs? In 2002, less than 20 percent of doctors had digitized their patients' medical records in any way. Even in 2010 only 11.5 percent of hospitals had implemented even the most basic digital record-keeping. Physician use of digital patient records to some degree had edged up to 13 percent. You may have seen these statistics as an illustration of the low adoption rate for electronic medical records—EMRs for short. But it's not the whole story, and the truth was even less heartening: According to research published in the *New England Journal of Medicine*,[10] as recently as 2008, just 2 percent of hospitals and 4 percent of doctors had a truly comprehensive electronic health record, or EHR, that integrated patient records, pharmacy prescribing, and the ability to incorporate test results from labs and scanning facilities. The rest were minimally digital—allowing doctors to prescribe via a computerized system, for example, or receive lab or radiology test results, or keep a patient's records in a computer without any other functionality. Basic, and a great start. But not fully electronic or ready to take advantage of all the capabilities that make EHRs a necessity for the practice of great twenty-first century medicine.

By 2011, the story became less grim. By then, about 57 percent of physicians were using at least the most basic EMR system. Hospitals were still in the 18 percent range for the most basic implementation of an EMR. (See Figure 1.1.) That's a terrific leap in the right direction. But even among

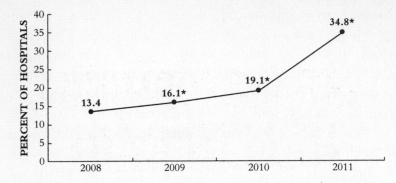

Figure 1.1 Hospital adoption of EHR systems has more than doubled since 2009.
SOURCE: ONC/American Hospital Association (AHA), AHA Annual Survey, Information Technology Supplement.

the most advanced systems, few have taken the steps to make the powerful move from EMR to EHR by connecting to other systems so specialists, hospitals, other healthcare practitioners, and patients can share and analyze information.

Who's gone electronic? At this point, it's younger doctors who work in the western United States, and early on it was doctors in big practices, according to Harvard Medical School researchers who studied EMR adoption in 2008. Among hospitals, large systems with connections to the academic world were early adopters. And since 2008, the groups most quickly adopting the most basic EHR system have continued to be younger, and have included primary care physicians and practices of three or more physicians.[11] (See Figure 1.2.)

Surveys done in 2012 show that the pace of EHR adoption has picked up considerably. And, like realtors who emphasize the importance of location, the adoption of EHR software in physician practices varies widely from state to state. (Table 1.1) Looking at EHR use by state reveals some surprises. In July 2012, two-thirds of physician practices in Minnesota and Utah were using EHR, with North

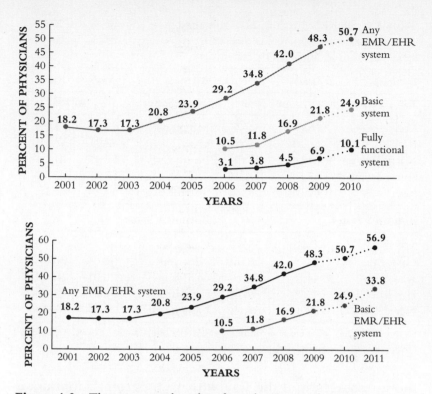

Figure 1.2 These two graphs, taken from the Centers for Disease Control's annual surveys of EHR adoption by office-based physicians, show steady progress. The majority of them now use EHRs.
SOURCE: CDC/NCHS, National Ambulatory Medical Care Survey.

and South Dakota and Iowa nearing that threshold, while less than half the physician practices in California, New York, New Jersey, Maryland, and Louisiana have adopted EHR software. This is most likely explained by the larger number of physician practices in those more populous states, but it also underscores the need to extend this valuable technological advance in every state.

Another gap reveals itself in an analysis of EMR adoption by practice size, although it too continues to narrow. (Table 1.2) It is not surprising that larger practices, with

Table 1.1 Published in July 2012, this chart gives an overview of how physician practices in individual states are progressing toward adoption of basic and more advanced EHR systems.

By State	Yes%	No%	By State	Yes%	No%
Top 5 States	July 2012		Top 5 States	Jan 2012	
Minnesota	68.6%	31.4%	Minnesota	65.2%	34.8%
Utah	66.8%	33.2%	Utah	62.7%	37.3%
North Dakota	64.0%	36.0%	North Dakota	59.9%	40.1%
South Dakota	62.3%	37.7%	Oregon	57.3%	42.7%
Iowa	61.2%	38.8%	South Dakota	57.2%	42.8%
Bottom 5 States			Bottom 5 States		
Maryland	44.4%	55.6%	California	40.1%	59.9%
California	44.0%	56.0%	New York	40.0%	60.0%
New York	43.5%	56.5%	Maryland	40.0%	60.0%
Louisiana	40.7%	59.3%	Louisiana	36.6%	63.4%
New Jersey	38.4%	61.6%	New Jersey	34.6%	65.4%

SOURCE: "Physician Office Usage of Electronic Health Records Software," SK&A, A Cegedim Company, Irvine, Calif. July 2012

more resources, lead the way with 78.8 percent adoption, it is heartening that nearly 53 percent of two-physician practices now use EMR software.

Broader adoption of both EHRs and EMRs is being spurred by $19 billion in federal stimulus funds announced by President Obama in 2009—and another $162 million added by Congress during the final days of the 2010 healthcare reform debate. Tapping these funds, states can funnel incentive grants to practitioners and hospitals ready to go digital before a 2014 deadline (Figure 1.3). Doctors can qualify for $44,000 to $64,000 in incentives; hospitals, several million dollars.

Naturally, this financial carrot-and-stick (offices that are not using EMRs in a meaningful way by the deadline will face reduced Medicare reimbursements) has spurred a flurry of activity as states, doctors, and healthcare systems get up

Table 1.2 Smaller physician practices lag in adopting electronic medical records, as a nationwide survey done in July 2012 by the market research firm SK&A shows.

By Number of Physicians at Site	July 2012		January 2012	
	Yes	No	Yes	No
1 physician	41.8%	58.2%	36.9%	63.1%
2 physicians	51.5%	48.5%	47.1%	52.9%
3–5 physicians	57.9%	42.1%	54.9%	45.1%
6–10 physicians	66.6%	33.4%	64.9%	35.1%
11–25 physicians	74.8%	25.2%	74.0%	26.0%
26 or more physicians	78.8%	21.2%	77.2%	22.8%

SOURCE: "Physician Office Usage of Electronic Health Records Software," SK&A, A Cegedim Company, Irvine, Calif. July 2012

to speed. At the same time, hundreds of tech companies—including titans like Intel, IBM, and General Electric, household names like Google and Microsoft, and vendors barely known outside the health IT world such as Meditech, McKesson Provider Tech, and Cerner—are clamoring for their business. And inside the health IT community, an extremely lively debate rages about the best way to usher this revolution into reality.

A Life-Saving Breakthrough

It's noisy out there—observers compare it to the Gold Rush of the 1800s. Yet most patients haven't heard much at all about EMRs—and their amazing potential.

I have to raise what, for me, is an obvious question: If electronic medical records were a new cancer drug or advanced medical imaging capability, would they be purchased throughout the healthcare system? Would they be on

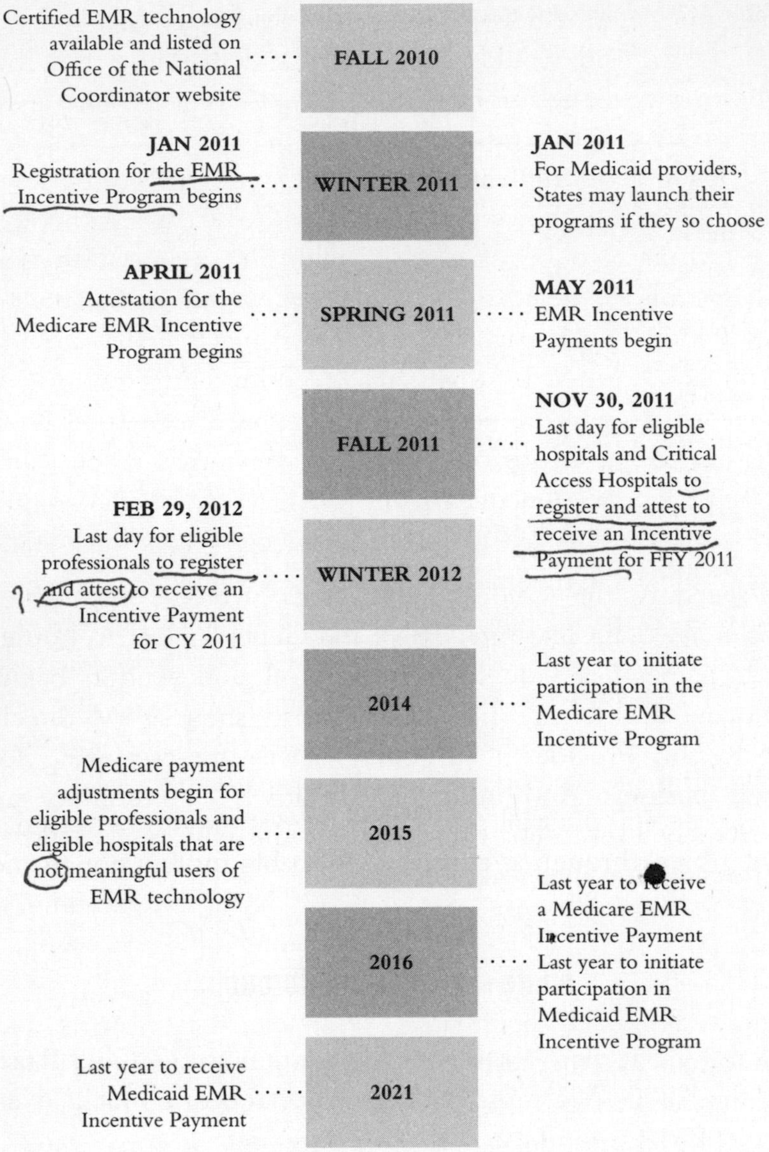

Certified EMR technology available and listed on Office of the National Coordinator website ····· **FALL 2010**

JAN 2011
Registration for the EMR Incentive Program begins ····· **WINTER 2011** ····· **JAN 2011** For Medicaid providers, States may launch their programs if they so choose

APRIL 2011
Attestation for the Medicare EMR Incentive Program begins ····· **SPRING 2011** ···· **MAY 2011** EMR Incentive Payments begin

FALL 2011 ····· **NOV 30, 2011** Last day for eligible hospitals and Critical Access Hospitals to register and attest to receive an Incentive Payment for FFY 2011

FEB 29, 2012
Last day for eligible professionals to register and attest to receive an Incentive Payment for CY 2011 ····· **WINTER 2012**

2014 ····· Last year to initiate participation in the Medicare EMR Incentive Program

Medicare payment adjustments begin for eligible professionals and eligible hospitals that are not meaningful users of EMR technology ····· **2015**

2016 ····· Last year to receive a Medicare EMR Incentive Payment / Last year to initiate participation in Medicaid EMR Incentive Program

Last year to receive Medicaid EMR Incentive Payment ····· **2021**

Figure 1.3   This time line shows key dates in the Medicare EMR Incentive Program, which is encouraging adoption of electronic medical records.
SOURCE: Optum Insight: www.optuminsight.com/emr-transition/overview/.

the front page of newspapers or the lead story on the evening news? And, would U.S. citizens be demanding they, too, receive their benefits? I believe in most cases the answer to each of these questions is yes.

But in the American healthcare system, people have not been given the choice when it comes to EMRs. Either we are fortunate to be part of a healthcare organization that has proactively decided to digitize, or we are still going to a provider who is part of a healthcare practice that has yet to be transformed by this great breakthrough. For most of us, unfortunately, the decision of when and how to digitize remains in the hands of those who still measure the value of a physician's practice by how many paper records fill the archives. This old measure of success became the standard by which the industry attributed value to a medical practice, and ultimately a retirement package for many. It still dogs us today, combined with the prevalent fee-for-service model in healthcare, where the more treatments and services a physician provides, the more successful her practice, whether the services result in healthier patients or not.

Electronic medical records are, in my opinion, as important a breakthrough as penicillin. Probably more. Though the United States leads the world in healthcare expenditures—$2.5 trillion in 2009 and rising every year—we ranked last in one study of medical outcomes in the world's most highly developed countries.[12] Digitizing healthcare could change all that, because it could identify and stop spending on unnecessary care (one Dartmouth College study suggests one-third of care delivered in the United States may not be truly needed). It can also flag killer errors—from dangerous prescription drug mistakes to tiny but important oversights while a patient's under anesthesia in the operating room, to missed screening tests for diabetes, colon cancer, and other conditions that needlessly drive up rates of advanced heart disease, diabetes, and cancer. An intelligent EHR system can remind patients of their next appointment and when it's time to take their medicine. And that is only the beginning. Once we are truly a digital industry, we can begin to use simple mathematics to analyze our records and assess conditions against a huge database of conditions. The potential is significant for caregivers and patients to improve health outcomes, from diagnosis and treatment to follow-up.

The interesting thing is, better health outcomes has been the dream driving innovation in patient record-keeping for over 100 years. In that sense, digital records aren't some strange and exotic new creature—they're the logical extension of a series of innovations in patient care stretching back to the days of our great-great-grandparents. What's new is that the technology now is available to make digital records and the tools that extend their value a reality. Having an EHR system available for the treatment of every patient in the United States, indeed the world, should be a right, not a privilege. Care providers should demand it. Patients should measure the care they receive based on it. And regulators should hold the entire industry accountable for the transition.

The Dawn of the Patient Record

In July of 1907, the Mayo Clinic in Rochester, Minnesota, assigned its first number to a patient—and changed medical history forever. Patient #1's records were dropped into a large paper envelope and filed away—a turning point in medical chart-keeping. Before, records at Mayo and in most other clinics were kept in a ledger that recorded all of a day's patient visits, one after another. Multiple ledgers were kept in different departments of the hospital, so just tracking down the right ledger and then piecing together a patient's history from entries on different pages was frustrating and time consuming.

Mayo's Henry S. Plummer, MD, introduced the new system, which still feels familiar today: Clinical visits, hospital stays, laboratory tests, and notes were put into a paper envelope marked with the patient's number. The envelopes were stored, in numerical order, in a central location. Later, conveyor belts and pneumatic tubes were added—inspired by their use in factories—to move the files more swiftly through the hospital. By 1930, standardized record sheets were introduced. Dr. Plummer is hailed as one of the greatest healthcare innovators of the early twentieth century, for good reason. Even today, the basic premises of his standardized records haven't changed: Complete information gathered in one file, easily accessible by others, and easily updated at each visit.

Today about 7 million clinic numbers have been assigned to 7 million Mayo Clinic patients. Yes, the Mayo Clinic now uses EMRs. But Plummer's record-keeping Big Idea is still at the heart of the system.[13]

It would take more than 60 years for the next Big Idea in medical charts to burst onto the scene—the electronic medical record. But it's still the exception, not the rule.

The Digital Age Dawns

In 1969, an article in the *British Medical Journal* warned readers not to be dazzled by a "new kind of machine, the electronic digital computer." The author, a physician and former medical records director of Glasgow University, noted that "Attempts are now being made to design computerized 'total information systems' ... and the possibility of automated diagnosis is being seriously discussed."[14]

But the revolution was already rolling—thanks to innovators who saw that computers weren't evil at all, but in fact had amazing potential to improve patient health. At the University of Vermont, Lawrence L. Weed, MD, was developing a system that organized records around a patient's various health problems (instead of chronologically)—and used a huge databank of medical information to inform doctors about best practices for diagnosis, treatment, and prevention of a patient's various conditions. Adopted in the early 1970s in some departments of the university's medical center, at East Maine General Hospital and in other medical centers, the system had an interactive touch screen where patients and nurses could input information that a doctor could then review. It sought to get beyond the limitations of a single physician's brain—and tap into a world of knowledge.[15]

Doctors who used the system, called problem-oriented medical records, loved it. Charles Burger, MD, a physician in Bangor, Maine, who began using Weed's system in the 1980s, told *The Economist* magazine that trying to treat patients without a computerized system is "like trying to send people up on the space shuttle with pencil and paper. There is no other profession that tries to operate in the fashion we do. We go on hallucinating about what we can do."[16]

Others saw the same promise in digitized records—and the same need to give physicians easy access not only to a patient's health information but also to an ever-expanding world of medical research and clinical guidelines. At nearly the same time, computerized patient charts were introduced at the Indiana University's Wishard Diabetes Clinic.[17] In 1988, doctors from the university reported in the *Journal of the American Medical Association* that "over the next few years, computer-stored medical records will become technically and economically feasible on a broad scale."[18] And they were. By 1994, EMRs were in use throughout Wishard Hospital—and linked to the emergency departments of 18 other Indianapolis hospitals in the nation's first citywide records system.[19, 20]

The rest of America was slower to respond. In 1999—when most Americans used computers at work and many had one at home as well—America's largest organization of family-practice doctors still saw computers in medicine as the wave of the future, not of the present. "Although progressing slowly, we will eventually see sophisticated clinical data systems in most practices," the American Academy of Family Physicians noted in a report about medical practice for the twenty-first century.[21]

Five years later, the horizon was pushed out a little further—and EMRs were still a rarity. In 2004, President George W. Bush said in his State of the Union address that every American needed to have an electronic medical record by the year 2014.

The Kaiser Permanente Experience

I have to stop right here to give credit where credit is due. I work for a great organization founded on the core principle that medicine should be practiced in such a way as to keep people healthy—to prevent bad outcomes from happening rather than waiting to treat them. This organization is Kaiser Permanente.

The seeds of the Kaiser Permanente medical program were sown in the hardscrabble years of the Great Depression and in the austere environs of the Mojave Desert. Here in 1933 a solo practitioner, Sidney R. Garfield, MD, developed a prepay plan with a modest payroll deduction to fund care for the workers engaged in the construction of the Colorado River Aqueduct. This experiment with prepayment brought quality medical care within the reach of the common man. And, somewhat troubled by the conventional practice of deriving income from illness and injury—and knowing that the workers wanted to stay well and on the job—Garfield encouraged workplace safety and the prevention of illness.

When Garfield's success in the desert was brought to Henry J. Kaiser's attention, the industrialist contracted with Garfield in 1938 to provide medical care for the Kaiser workforce at the Grand Coulee Dam in Washington state. Here the two began to dream of assembling a robust medical care program built on the utility of prepayment, with physicians organized in group practice as found in university teaching hospitals, and with modern clinics and hospitals funded through the modest prepay dollar. This innovative system for health care was born in the Kaiser WWII shipyards and steel mills in 1942 and opened to the public in 1945. Early member groups included municipal employees, university faculty and staff, and labor unions.

In 1950, health plan membership grew dramatically when the leaders of the International Longshoremen's and Warehousemen's Union (ILWU) enrolled the union's chapters on the entire west coast. The study of routine processes in an annual health checkup for this large member group led to early initiatives in medical informatics, and eventually to Kaiser Permanente's leadership in the development of the electronic health record. Garfield, with Dr. Morris F. Collen, a pioneer in medical informatics, published widely in the medical literature in the 1960s their vision for the electronic health record in the hospital of the future.

Today, Kaiser Permanente's more than 16,000 doctors and 37 hospitals serve nine million members in nine states and the District of Columbia. We have the benefits of great founding principles coupled with great care and supported by advances in information technology. And the results are even more remarkable. For example:

- In 2002, Kaiser Permanente's preventive-care services in northern California reduced deaths from heart disease (the nation's leading cause of death) by 73 percent— a drop so significant that coronary artery disease was no longer the top cause of mortality for our 3 million northern California members, according to the non-profit National Committee for Quality Assurance. The reason? Team-based medicine and computer-supported care registries tracked patient health during and after hospital stays, comparing treatments and outcomes to national guidelines and to best practices in medicine. We increased cholesterol screenings in cardiac patients from 55 to 97 percent and boosted the number who met healthy cholesterol targets from 26 to 73 percent. That's crucial, because high levels of LDL cholesterol jump-start the process that clogs arteries in the heart with gunky, perilous plaque.[22, 23]
- Using technology, we increased breast cancer screenings 11 percent, saving an estimated 550 lives across the system. Colon cancer screening increased 23 percent, saving 3,664 lives.[24]

Doctors in our hospitals can check your full health record anywhere, any time—no need to rush to the nurse's station in the hospital or run to the records room in the office. At Kaiser Permanente, we have 5,000 mobile computers— dubbed WOW carts, for Workstation on Wheels[25]—so the p.18 volunteers for research

info's available bedside or during a test or procedure. We are beginning to deploy tablets, such as iPads, to help care teams on the go and at the side of a patient's bed capture and access the information they need to provide the best quality care. In the homes of our members, digitized healthcare means logging on to find local farmers' markets carrying seasonal produce, letting their kids play an award-winning (and fun) healthy-food video game, and going online to schedule appointments, refill prescriptions, e-mail their doctor (yes, the doctors write back). Our members checked nearly 30 million lab tests online in 2011 alone.[26]

Digital health has huge potential for even better things. With a $25 million grant from the National Institutes of Health, we are now establishing a research database with genetic, health, lifestyle, and environmental information from 100,000 subscribers. They've all volunteered to give saliva samples for genetic testing and have opened their health records to scientists. Researchers everywhere will have access to the database, to answer questions such as how genes influence a drug's effect on the body and why the health of people with heart disease and diabetes can deteriorate so rapidly.[27]

Electronic Health Records: All You, All Digital

The first step on the road to preventive care for all? Secure, confidential, accessible electronic health information. Everyone practicing medicine and every hospital will need to have an electronic system for medical record-keeping. It need not be a universal system, although that would help. Getting disparate systems to talk with each other, within or among care settings, is a challenge, but several organizations are making strides on that front, too. Maintaining basic health information about patients is table stakes in the future of preventive care, and the entire game depends on it.

The information stored on your behalf will, in most cases, go far beyond the scattered factoids that make up your records now. Paper medical record-keeping isn't really designed with preventive care in mind; more often it's simply a snapshot of your visits, a way to set codes for billing, and as backup in the event your doctor is ever sued. In contrast, an electronic health record (EHR) capable of delivering preventive care must include your family and personal medical histories, past test results, X-rays and scans, drug history including reactions and interactions, allergies, and other relevant information such as environmental or job exposures to toxins.

Of course, this information must be secure to protect your privacy and your rights. Patient data represents the ultimate prize for attackers and malicious users in the online world. There are too many hackers and people seeking to exploit this highly personal information. We also will have to look at how to best control who can see information and for what purpose. We would not, for example, want to create situations where people could be discriminated against based on information stored in the EMR. From its inception, the medical profession has held doctor-patient confidentiality as sacrosanct. It is even protected by our legal system. I am certain that our physicians and patients would not let those of us in the health IT community get away with anything less than scrupulous attention to data security at every step in this process. Nor should they.

With good, secure information in place, software in your doctor's computer system can search your record for red flags. Is your blood pressure inching up? Have your levels of protective "good" cholesterol fallen? Did you forget to fill your cholesterol prescription? Skip your visit with the nutritionist? Are you overdue for a flu vaccine? Is your weight creeping up? Once alerted, your doctor can take steps to avert health problems at an earlier stage than ever before.

EHRs are proven health promoters. When the Cleveland Clinic installed an electronic system, the institution saw major improvements precisely because doctors were alerted to gaps in patient care. Pneumonia vaccines for elderly and sick patients rose from 73 to 90 percent. Bone density scan rates increased from 61 to 85 percent and mammogram use saw a similar rise.[28]

A thorough EHR helped some Massachusetts smokers kick the habit. At the Harvard Medical School–affiliated Brigham and Women's Hospital in Boston, adding smoking status information to EHRs meant patients were 10 times more likely to be referred to a smoking cessation counselor—and 2½ times more likely to be successful quitters nine months later.[29]

Tied to your cell phone and even to your Twitter account, your EHR can nudge you to do the right things for your health even when your doctor is not around. University of California, Davis researchers tweeted "use your sunscreen" messages to half of a group of 70 study volunteers in a study, then tracked how much sunscreen they actually used by attaching sensors to bottles of sun block. The Twitter group was twice as likely to slather up—a move that reduces skin cancer significantly.[30]

Are we there yet? No. But the time's coming closer thanks to stimulus-fund incentives and some nuts-and-bolts developments that will make it easier for physicians and hospitals to take the plunge. Software for EMR systems is dropping in price—good news for doctors in smaller practices.

hich Time-saving new ways for doctors to input data (such as voice recognition software) are now part of some packages. And more sophisticated multitasking systems are available that couple record-keeping with other functions such as e-prescribing.

The next big thing could well be what people are calling "big data." This includes using large databases and care registries to amass and analyze massive amounts of data, searching for breakthroughs in the treatment, prevention, or prediction of illness. It also includes the integration of data from outside the healthcare setting—say, a personal health record maintained by an individual—into that person's electronic medical record.

From the Back Office to Better Health

Of course, anyone who's ever scheduled a medical appointment or had to wrangle over a hospital bill knows that computers have been a staple in doctors' offices and hospitals for about two decades now. They've supported the billing department—helping staff keep track of an ever-changing maze of billing codes and insurance company reimbursement rules. Computers are also way better than a paper appointment book for riding herd on the complexities of coordinating doctors' schedules with patients' busy lives.

But these computers don't change the quality of care patients receive. That is dictated by the training your doctor received in medical school and her subsequent experience as a practitioner, by her access to high-quality medical facilities and devices, by her ability to consult with specialists, and by her dedication to keeping up with the latest developments.

Most of us look to our physicians expecting they are all-knowing. We trust their personal knowledge and experience will be sufficient to take care of our problem. The fundamental question that should be asked is: Is this the best we can do? Physicians are required to use what they learn in medical school throughout their entire career. And then to supplement it with what they are individually able to read each year and their personal experience. Few would argue with the assertion that the knowledge of many physicians is better than the knowledge of one alone. No one can keep up with the trove of knowledge necessary in present-day medicine without support. Some of that support has to come from automated medical records and journals. Physicians need an intelligent stream of research findings and evolving medical information. Technology has been widely adopted almost everywhere else, improving precision, performance, and quality along the way. It is essential in healthcare too.

Healthcare institutions that have taken the next step by digitizing the thousands or even millions of paper charts in the records room are seeing payoffs in terms of better outcomes for their patients. As these systems have become more sophisticated, they have not only automated the medical record, they have created the ability to integrate all information about a particular patient, his full health history, laboratory tests, prescriptions, illnesses, family history, and so on. It incorporates all the little, and in many cases very relevant, details about the person. These systems can also carry notes on standards of care, common practices, drug interactions, and many other useful reminders for caregivers.

The payback for patients has been better health.

- **Healthcare despite disaster**. In the aftermath of Hurricane Katrina, one group of New Orleans evacuees didn't lose access to their medical records: the 50,000 veterans who were patients of the Southeast Louisiana

VA

Veterans Health Care System. Three days after the storm hit the Gulf Coast, a Veterans Affairs Department computer specialist was airlifted out of New Orleans with backup tapes of all local records. By the next evening, the records had been plugged into VA computers in Houston, Texas. Flood victims who fled to 48 states and the District of Columbia thereby had access to up to 20 years of lab results and six years' worth of X-rays, scans, doctors' notes, and medication records. By late September of 2005, a month after the storm hit, 15,000 displaced veterans had used the system.[31, 32]

nice example

- **Smarter care for chronic medical conditions**. The Marshfield Clinic in Marshfield, Wisconsin, first installed an EMR system in 1985 and went fully digital by 2007—eliminating paper charts. The system included medical-alerting software that told doctors when patients had missed key tests and exams. Clinical researchers report that the system boosted the number of people with diabetes who received all important chronic-care services (including foot checks, flu shots, and A1C tests of long-term blood sugar control) from zero in 2004 to 47 percent by 2008. And for heart patients taking the tricky-to-manage anticlotting drug warfarin, a computerized monitoring system worked so well that it reduced hospital stays by 41 percent, saving Medicare $9,443 for each hospitalization that didn't happen.[33]

warfarin

- **Avoiding fractured bones—and fractured lives**. At Kaiser Permanente, a computerized outreach program improved care for thousands of women and men who'd had bone fractures due to osteoporosis. Across its clinics, the alerting system improved evaluation and treatment of brittle-bone disease by up to 44 percent—reducing the high risk for subsequent fractures. "Osteoporosis now causes more deaths annually than breast cancer and ovarian cancer combined," notes Adrianne Feldstein, MD, MS, an investigator at the Kaiser Permanente Center for Health Research in Portland and the lead author of the study. "This study shows that we can cost-effectively improve management with interventions as simple as e-mails, letters and phone calls. That in turn should reduce fractures and mortality, and improve quality of life."[34]

- **Safer anesthesia care.** Starting in 2003 anesthesiologists at Massachusetts General Hospital in Boston used a data bank of over 500,000 digital surgery records to study rare side effects of anesthesia. They used the information to build a system that notifies doctors of anesthesia-related problems in real time—during surgery. It's paying off. In a recent study involving several hospitals, a notification system helped anesthesiologists spot potential problems early and improve care on the spot.[35]

What's ahead? When economists from the RAND Corporation looked at the potential health benefits of EHRs for the entire nation, their estimates were staggering

- **2.2 million fewer drug errors.** If hospitals and doctors adopted EHRs that included software to flag potential drug interactions and reactions, this huge category of preventable medical errors could be slashed significantly, the researchers said. This would save lives and money—an estimated $4.5 billion to be precise.[36]
- **Life-saving healthcare basics.** Using EHRs to find the millions of people over age 65 who aren't receiving recommended vaccinations against influenza and pneumonia could save 20,000 to 38,000 lives a year, the RAND analysts report.[37] EHRs could also alert those who haven't received recommended screenings for breast

and colon cancer. By detecting more cancers in earlier treatable stages, many lives could be saved.

Given data like these, in any other industry there would be government committees set up to review why more progress hasn't been made. The public outcry would be deafening. Public service campaigns would be launched targeting care providers. If you're over 35, you probably remember Smokey the Bear with his authoritative call to action, "Only you can prevent forest fires." And we did prevent wildfires: The Forest Fire Prevention campaign reports that this campaign helped reduce the number of acres lost annually from 22 million when it first hit the airwaves in 1944 to 8.4 million in 2000. And yet the health care–consuming public knows very little about the state of EHRs in the industry and the resulting health outcomes and lives that this technology in the hands of skilled physicians can save. We need to mobilize healthcare providers and consumers with the message that they can influence the future of healthcare IT.

From Paper to EMRs to EHRs to the Future

In their day, paper medical files represented a giant step forward in health care. Their day has passed. Today's electronic medical records are measured in megabits, not pages. EMRs are more accurate, efficient, and comprehensive. Their adoption by physicians (57 percent) and hospitals (18 percent) is growing, fueled in part by new products being developed by leading health care technology developers. But we cannot transform healthcare using EMRs; that requires a more powerful tool: the electronic health record.

I consider EHRs as important a contribution to public health as penicillin. These records, which compile information from across an organization, and more importantly, can be shared among healthcare organizations, can help us avoid redundant testing, prevent medication errors, and save lives. Kaiser Permanente has proven this. We have harnessed the data in the EHRs of our 8.9 million members to reduce deaths from heart disease and to increase life-saving breast cancer screenings.

If done poorly, health IT could do more harm than good. Systems could fail to communicate reliably or at all. Without impeccable security built in, patients' information could be taken advantage of by unscrupulous outsiders. But I doubt that will be the case in the big picture. For one thing, as I will discuss in coming chapters, we have some good models to build on and skilled innovators eager to engage in this exciting challenge. We have good partners in government and the healthcare and IT communities. Most of all, we all have a stake in the success of this endeavor.

Notes

1. Regina Holliday story: www.youtube.com/watch?v=msBYOYYeHPw.

2. K. S. Dawes, "Survey of General Practice Records," *British Medical Journal* 3 (1972): 219–223. As described in Institute of Medicine, *The Computer-Based Patient Record: An Essential Technology for Health Care*, rev. ed. (Washington, DC: The National Academies Press, 1997), 60, http://books.nap.edu/openbook.php?isbn=0309055326&page=60.

3. John F. Burnum, "The Misinformation Era: The Fall of the Medical Record," *Annals of Internal Medicine* 110, no. 6 (March 1989), http://annals.org/article.aspx?volume=110&page=482.

    As quoted in Institute of Medicine, *The Computer-Based Patient Record: An Essential Technology for Health Care*, rev. ed. (Washington, DC: The National Academies Press, 1997), 58, http://books.google.com/books?id=AZ_Ia21-BosC&pg=PA58&lpg=PA58&dq=medical+records,+which+have+long+been+faulty,+

contain+more+distorted,+deleted,+and+misleading+inform
ation+than+ever+before&source=bl&ots=is2FiagFyk&sig=B
ZCctfToYboqZwoU7RE4vkrfY1k&hl=en&sa=X&ei=ibwKU
KCoB4nm6gGKiv2lCg&ved=0CFEQ6AEwAQ#v=onepage
&q=medical%20records%2C%20which%20have%20long%20
been%20faulty%2C%20contain%20more%20distorted%2C%20delet-
ed%2C%20and%20misleading%20information%20than%20ever%20
before&f=false.

4. Anne Bruner, "Handwriting Errors: Harmful, Wasteful and
Preventable," *Journal of the Kentucky Medical Association* 99, no. 5
(May 2001):189–192, www.kyma.org/uploads/file/patient_safety/
physicians/harmful_wasteful_and_preventable.pdf.

5. "Putting It on Paper," *Wall Street Journal*, April 6, 1992. Cited in
"ICU Clinical Information Management System: An Investigation
for a Pediatric Intensive Care Unit," www.andrew.cmu.edu/
course/90-853/medis.dir/.../picuemr.doc.

6. Richard Pizzi, "Gulf Coast Clinics Move to Digitize Records
Post-Katrina," *HealthcareIT News*, September 18, 2007, www.med-
comsoft.com/documents/Gulf-Coast-clinics-move-to-digitize-
records-post-Katrina.pdf.

7. Jolt Roukema, "Paper versus Computer: Feasibility of an Electronic
Medical Record in General Pediatrics," *Pediatrics* 117, no. 1 (January
1, 2006), www.pediatricsdigest.mobi/content/117/1/15.full.

8. "EMR vs. EHR – What is the Difference?" January 4, 2011. U.S.
Department of Health & Human Services, Office of the National
Coordinator for Health Information Technology, www.healthit
.gov/buzz-blog/electronic-health-and-medical-records/
emr-vs-ehr-difference/.

9. Ibid.

10. "Electronic Health Records in Ambulatory Care—A National
Survey of Physicians," *New England Journal of Medicine* 359, no. 1
(2008): 50–60, www.nejm.org/doi/full/10.1056/NEJMsa0802005.

11. C. M. DesRoches, M. W. Painter, and A. K. Jha, *Health Information
Technology in the United States: Driving toward Delivery System Change*
(Robert Wood Johnson Foundation, Harvard School of Public
Health and Mathematical Policy Research, 2012).

12. Ellen Nolte and C. Martin McKee, "Variations in Amenable Mortality—Trends in 16 High-Income Nations," *Health Policy*, September 12, 2011, www.commonwealthfund.org/~/media/Files/Publications/In%20the%20Literature/2011/Sep/1549_Nolte_variations_amenable_mortality_HltPolicy_09122011_ITL_v4.pdf.

13. Mayo Clinic, *Medical Records at Mayo*, www.mayoclinic.org/tradition-heritage/medical-records.html.

14. J. H. Mitchell, "Relevance of the Electronic Computer to Hospital Medical Records," *British Medical Journal*, October 18, 1969, www.bmj.com/content/4/5676/157.abstract.

15. Lee Jacobs, "Interview with Lawrence Weed, MD—The Father of the Problem-Oriented Medical Record Looks Ahead," *Permanente Journal* 13, no. 3 (Summer 2009): 84–89, www.ncbi.nlm.nih.gov/pmc/articles/PMC2911807/?tool=pubmed.

16. "Brain Scan: The Computer Will See You Now," *The Economist*, December 8, 2005, www.economist.com/node/5269189.

17. Patrick J. McGinnis, "The Scope and Direction of Health Informatics," NASA Johnson Space Center, Medical Operations Branch, http://ntrs.nasa.gov/archive/nasa/casi.ntrs.nasa.gov/20100036414_2010036852.pdf.

18. C. J. McDonald, "Computer-Stored Medical Records: Their Future Role in Medical Practice," *Journal of the American Medical Association* 259, no. 23 (June 1988): 3433–3440.

19. Regenstrief Institute, Inc., *Advancing Healthcare through Research, Development, and Education*, www.regenstrief.org/.

20. Indiana Network for Patient Care, *Supporting Clinical Care through Health Information Exchange*, www.regenstrief.org/medinformatics/inpc/.

21. American Academy of Family Physicians 1997–1998 Task Force to Enhance Family Practice Research, *Practice-Based Research Networks in the 21st Century: The Pearls of Research* (Leawood, KS: American Academy of Family Physicians, 1999): 123, www.aafp.org/online/etc/medialib/aafp_org/documents/clinical/research/pbrns21st.Par.0001.File.tmp/pbrnconfproc.pdf.

22. Rachael King, "CEO Guide to Technology: How Kaiser Permanente Went Paperless," *BusinessWeek*, April 07, 2009, www.businessweek. com/technology/content/apr2009/tc2009047_562738.htm.

23. Kaiser Permanente, *Case Study: Collaborative Cardiac Care Service—Collaborative Teams Improve Cardiac Care with Health Information Technology*, March 27, 2009, http://xnet.kp.org/future/ahrstudy/032709cardiac.html.

24. Patty Enrado, "Kaiser IT Initiatives Ready for Pilots, Rollout," *HealthcareIT News*, April 22, 2009, www.healthcareitnews.com/news/kaiser-it-initiatives-ready-pilots-rollout.

25. CBS News, *Charting a New Course*, September 14, 2009, www .cbsnews.com/2100-3445_162-5306927.html.

26. Kaiser Permanente, *Kaiser Permanente Honored as Leader in Health Information Technology*, April 6, 2009, http://xnet.kp.org/newscenter/pressreleases/nat/2009/040609himssstage7.html.

27. David Talbot, "Massive Gene Database Planned in California," *MIT Technology Review*, October 21, 2009, www.technologyreview.com/news/415914/massive-gene-database-planned-in-california/.

28. Emma Schwartz, "Can Cleveland Clinic Be a Model for Digital Medicine?" *Huffington Post Investigative Fund*, March 18, 2010, www.huffingtonpost.com/2009/12/02/can-cleveland-clinic-be-a_n_376842.html.

29. J. A. Linder, "An Electronic Health Record-Based Intervention to Improve Tobacco Treatment in Primary Care: A Cluster-Randomized Controlled Trial," *Archives of Internal Medicine* 169, no. 8 (April 2009): 781–787, www.ncbi.nlm.nih.gov/pmc/articles/PMC3005286/?tool=pubmed.

30. April W. Armstrong, "Text-Message Reminders to Improve Sunscreen Use: A Randomized, Controlled Trial Using Electronic Monitoring," *Archives of Dermatology* 145, no. 11 (2009): 1230–1236, http://archderm.jamanetwork.com/article.aspx?articleid=712278.

31. Associated Press, "Katrina Highlights Need for Computerized Health Records," *USA Today*, September 13, 2005, www.usatoday.com/news/health/2005-09-13-karina-health-records_x.htm.

32. *Hurricane Katrina: A Nation Still Unprepared*. Special Report of the Committee on Homeland Security and Governmental Affairs, United States Senate, www.gpo.gov/fdsys/pkg/CRPT-109srpt322/pdf/CRPT-109srpt322.pdf.

33. Douglas McCarthy, "Marshfield Clinic: Health Information Technology Paves the Way for Population Health Management," The Commonwealth Fund, www.commonwealthfund.org/~/media/Files/Publications/Case%20Study/2009/Aug/1293_McCarthy_Marshfield_case_study.pdf.

34. Kaiser Permanente, *Kaiser Permanente Study Shows Electronic Medical Records and Outreach Improve Osteoporosis Care*, October 22, 2007, http://xnet.kp.org/newscenter/pressreleases/nat/2007/071022osteo.html.

35. Massachusetts General Hospital, *Electronic Charting and Process Control*, http://www2.massgeneral.org/anesthesia/index.aspx?page=research_biomedical&subpage=echarting2.

36. RAND Corporation, "Widespread Adoption of Health Information Technology Could Save $162 Billion a Year, Says RAND Study, but the Federal Government Needs to Help," September 14, 2005, www.healthaffairs.org/press/septoct0501.htm.

37. Richard Hillestad, "Can Electronic Medical Record Systems Transform Health Care? Potential Health Benefits, Savings, and Costs," *Health Affairs* 24, no. 5 (September 2005): 1103–1117.

Chapter 2

The Future

Health Information Exchanges and Health Financial Exchanges

An unconscious woman is rushed to the emergency room of Wishard Memorial Hospital in Indianapolis—and attending physician John T. Finnell has little to go on. The woman is 40 years old. She collapsed in the waiting room of one of the hospital's outpatient clinics. He knows her name. And that's all.

Finnell needs more information, fast. The woman's paper chart would take hours or even days to arrive. Thanks to the hospital system's interconnected electronic health record system, he's got the facts in less than a minute: The woman has a seizure disorder and had not been taking her medications. The details allow Finnell to deliver the care she needs.

Without lightning-fast access to vital data, the doctor would have resorted to Plan B: Giving the woman drugs to temporarily halt her breathing, inserting a breathing tube, ordering dozens of blood tests—then waiting for results that would tell him what was really going on. These measures would waste valuable minutes or even hours and could have had dire complications, including brain damage. When you're in an emergency and you can't find information about a patient, everybody suffers," Finnell says.

nice

In Indianapolis—one of the nation's most wired-for-health cities—quick saves like this are commonplace. Since 1997, five major hospital groups there have shared patient information in a groundbreaking collaboration called the Indianapolis Network for Patient Care. Since then, it has grown to include hospitals and doctor's offices across Indiana and beyond. In September of 2009, the Indiana Health Information Exchange "shook hands" with similar systems in Cincinnati, Ohio, and Bloomington, Indiana—and now links up 58 hospitals and 14,000 healthcare practitioners. Health insurance giants Anthem Blue Cross and Blue Shield and United Healthcare are involved, too, using digital medical records to better track patient health.[1]

Health information exchanges (HIEs) like this one allow for the fast, accurate transmission of electronic health data between doctors, hospitals, emergency rooms, labs, and patients themselves. They unlock the full potential of EMRs. And someday soon, the connections will be nationwide. *No*

We can thank the federal government for this, at least in part. More than $19 billion in federal incentives to doctors and hospitals will help push this important development. Not only will it fund the purchase and setup of EMRs, it

but only in condition of meaningful use

will encourage connection. The Federal HITECH Act calls for creation of 70 or more "regional health IT extension centers" that could help promote linkages by giving physicians "technical assistance, guidance, and information on best practices that support and accelerate health care providers' efforts to become meaningful users of Electronic Health Records (EHRs)."[2] And those who receive incentive grants must show they're making meaningful use of their new EMR systems—which will likely include a strong suggestion that systems learn how to talk to one another.

So we're on the way. But we should be ready for some inevitable—and surmountable—bumps in the road. Fortunately, we have some great examples of early adopters here, and in other parts of the world, to light the way.

Jumping the Hurdles

There are hurdles to implementing these systems: Cost. Time. The challenge of finding the right system. And the effort it takes to make the mental leap into a digital world. Jump those hurdles and there will inevitably be another: Computers aren't perfect. Stuff happens.

But it's worth forging ahead. Kaiser Permanente tried several paths before hitting on the route that led to our groundbreaking KP HealthConnect® system. Early on, we developed, then scrapped, a $400 million IT project. Along the way we frustrated our doctors and staff who had to learn new systems. We coped with decreased productivity and frustrating system outages. Installing an electronic health record isn't easy. But for every doctor who struggled, we had many more who passionately embraced the change because they were confident in its potential. Today, our caregivers have secure access to the health information of more than 9 million Kaiser Permanente members through KP HealthConnect. And each of those members can securely contact their care teams and look up their own health information through the kp.org website. In 2011 alone, Kaiser Permanente members viewed more than 29.7 million test results and sent more than 12 million secure e-mails to their physicians using My Health Manager on kp.org.

Ultimately, the biggest challenges go beyond software and dollars. Health IT has to prove, to doctors and patients, that it's safe, trustworthy, and better than that familiar manila folder. I think we're on the way.

Just Connect

In an age where healthcare is, in fact, real-time, information about every encounter with the healthcare system will be recorded in electronic files in a data center, entrusted to your healthcare provider or organization. Over time, you will visit numerous providers such as your primary care physician, specialist, allergist, and possibly a hospital. Today most of them keep paper files. In the future, your records will undoubtedly be electronic, as a medical or health record on each of their independent systems. Clearly better, it informs your physician about your health history, allergies, indications, and such. But so far, isolated EMRs simply eliminate paper records.

This next step—the HIE—may be a system that translates between separate electronic records kept in physicians' offices and in hospitals. Or it may function as a central data bank where doctors and hospitals can access a single, shared set of charts. It may also be a hybrid of the two. In any case,

HIEs will be the healthcare industry's go-between. Once created, they will make it possible for your specialist to consult your primary care physician's notes, assess your history, determine medial needs, and never have to ask you to fill out another frustrating questionnaire.

HIEs will enable the secure flow of your medical information between healthcare providers to whom you permit access. They will also provide you, the patient, with the ability to aggregate your own health information and make available to your team the exercise regimen you are following, your weight, diet, information about your stress levels, and more, so that your care providers can factor these into their assessment of your health and treatment of conditions you may have.

In other words, as Kaiser Permanente's CEO George Halvorson likes to say, "this disconnected non-system" we have now may ultimately become a truly connected system of care, operating efficiently on your behalf.

Lonely EMRs

Where do we stand right now? Remember that just 57 percent of doctors and 18 percent of hospitals use a basic EMR (electronic medical record) system. But only a handful can share information outside their own systems, through an electronic health record (EHR) that integrates with laboratory or pharmacy systems so physicians can easily see their patients' lab results and prescription records. As of February 2012, just 66 hospitals in the nation had been acknowledged with the coveted Stage 7 Award by the Healthcare Information and Management Systems Society for reaching the highest level of connectivity. These include Citizens Memorial Hospital in Bolivar, Missouri; North Shore

University Health System in Evanston, Illinois; Children's Hospital of Pittsburgh; and 36 hospitals that are part of Kaiser Permanente, headquartered in Oakland, California.[3]

There are HIEs organized by individual states as well, like the Indiana Health Information Exchange. In Delaware, a statewide health information network provides lab results, radiology reports, admissions/discharge/transfer records, and medication history information to doctors and pharmacists. The system recently added new capabilities: Doctors can enter treatment orders for hospitalized patients electronically, for example. And for the first time, the U.S. military is linking up two crucial sets of medical records. Veterans Affairs and the Department of Defense have joined forces to create a Joint Virtual Lifetime Electronic Record that will follow service members from enlistment through their postmilitary days if they receive care through the Veterans Administration.

Five leading health systems, each a pioneer in the use of electronic medical records for their patients, joined together in 2011 to form the Care Connectivity Consortium™ (CCC). Kaiser Permanente is one of those five organizations, along with Geisinger Health System, Mayo Clinic, Intermountain Healthcare, and Group Health Cooperative. The CCC aims to deliver patient-centered, community-wide, evidence-based care coordination, supported by timely information exchanged across the health care ecosystem regardless of organizational boundaries. The work is fueled only by the commitment and limited, though not insignificant, financial resources of the collective group. And in less than a year, the CCC began successfully sharing data across 13,000 care team providers from these five different organizations.

The CCC has had to overcome technical challenges—most notably the need to connect disparate EMR systems, ensure correct matching of patient records across organizations, and expand the clinical data content exchanged—all while adhering to national standards. To overcome the challenge of connecting different EMR systems, the CCC implemented health information exchange gateways that are fully compliant with specifications for the federal exchange. The gateways use standard electronic document formats in the exchange of health summary records. And there is technical design work that each organization had to perform on their individual EMR systems to make data sharing possible or more comprehensive.

The consortium continues to collaborate on building a shared service that will provide unique identity resolution and matching to ensure individuals are correctly authenticated and the right records are matched to the right patient—something we all will be grateful for as the collaboration develops. There will be work to expand the clinical data content exchanged to include immunizations, clinical lab results, vital signs, radiology reports, and hospital discharge summary reports.

It's challenging, but the CCC has demonstrated what can be done—and how quickly—when we have the common goal of doing the right thing for the patient.

Health information exchanges like these are still rare, for many reasons.

Money is a major factor. So is the fact that systems made by different manufacturers usually lack the capability to connect easily (a concept called interoperability). And the concept of working with competing hospitals or the doctors' group down the street is a new one: Hospitals and doctor's offices typically operate in a vacuum, making decisions (such as the purchase of an EMR system) based on their own needs—not the needs of a larger group. Add to that another big gap: a lack of industry-wide standards to ensure that shared data is accurate, up-to-date, accessible, and secure. From consumers, there's been understandable concern about privacy and security, too.

So if your local hospital or doctor's office isn't connected to others in your area, you're not alone. You're in good company. Some of the biggest, most advanced medical systems in the nation aren't linked. As of early 2010, Harvard University's two largest teaching hospitals could not exchange patient medical information, even though both institutions have advanced in-house electronic records systems. In Seattle, three of Washington state's top medical centers are located within walking distance of one another, yet despite state-of-the-art EMRs the hospitals cannot exchange health information about their patients. The reason? The systems were made by different manufacturers.

"A patient crossing the street from one hospital to another would be wise to take paper records," one news story noted.

Patient-Centered Care

HIEs make so much sense because they keep the focus on the patient. When all of your data is in one place, care improves. In fact, it can be revolutionized. Family doctors are excited about a new concept in care called the patient-centered medical home, in which doctors and other healthcare practitioners such as dietitians, physical therapists, diabetes educators, specialists, as well as hospitals, clinics, and nursing homes work together to coordinate the best care possible for each person. A medical home, a phrase introduced by the American Academy of Pediatrics back in 1967, gives your primary care doctor a central role in organizing care that may be delivered by a number of specialists and in different settings.

With a medical home, the emphasis shifts to preventive care. And a growing number of Americans with more than one chronic condition can finally receive care that makes sense. No more need to coordinate, on your own, medical records from a dozen or more doctors, to try to remember to tell each one about all of the medications you take, to be sure you're getting all the tests you need to stay healthy, and aren't taking expensive tests you've already taken.

It takes a good EMR system to make the medical home concept work. At the Group Health Cooperative, a Seattle-based nonprofit healthcare system, a medical home pilot project at its 9,200-patient Factoria Medical Center delivered great results for patients and doctors, thanks to EMRs and a reorganized care plan. Doctors spent more time with patients, held daily conferences to discuss the health of the previous day's patients (where they referred to patients' EMRs), collaborated more often with other practitioners, and focused more of their efforts on preventive health care. In one year, medical-home patients had 29 percent fewer emergency room visits than patients of the cooperative's traditional medical practices. Healthcare professionals felt less burned out. Just 10 percent felt emotionally exhausted, compared to 30 percent in traditional practices.[4]

Health Care Just Got Smarter

Hospitals in the EMR and HIE vanguard are finding that being connected is good for patients in many ways:

- **Fewer medication errors**. Citizens Memorial Healthcare in Bolivar, Missouri, went paperless in 2007 with a system that links emergency services, home care, hospice, long-term care, assisted living, same-day surgery, cancer care, rural health clinics, and family doctors, specialists, pharmacists, and patients. Computerized medication orders plus barcodes that match drug names, dosages, and timing with a patient's bar-coded records contributed to a 70 percent reduction in reported medication errors in the hospital.[5]

- **Coordinated care**. At the Children's Hospital of Pittsburgh, kids with complex medical needs may see up to 70 different healthcare practitioners during a hospital stay. Integrated, digital medical records do away with the risk of mistakes possible when treatment orders are given verbally or scrawled hastily in a chart or on a prescription pad. Orders for new drugs are recorded in patient charts in as little as 10 to 15 minutes, rather than taking more than an hour as they did in the days of paper files. A pediatrician can see the results of a young patient's latest lab test or radiology images at a child's bedside, while working in her office, or between patient visits in the hospital's outpatient clinics. This gets rid of waste two ways—saving time and reducing the need for duplicated tests and imaging when the first can't be found.[6]

- **Customized treatments**. In the greater Cincinnati area, linked EMRs allow sharing of health information and health tools among 29 hospitals, over 4,400 doctors, 17 health departments, as well as nursing homes, labs, and other parts of the healthcare community. Research conducted by the University of Cincinnati demonstrates the potential. Scientists looked at a computerized "decision support tool" that helped doctors assess whether patients were good candidates for the drug warfarin. Picking the right patients is crucial, because this powerful anticlotting drug can prevent strokes, but also raises risk for dangerous bleeding within the brain. In a study of over 6,000 people from various hospitals in the health system, they found that the tool accurately chose the best candidates for the drug—their side effect rates were about one-third lower than those advised not to use the medication.[7]

The Road Ahead

Even the most enthusiastic supporters of HIEs say linking up systems is not a task for the faint of heart. Hospitals that worked together to develop Indianapolis's medical data exchange admit that project nearly failed three separate times. Hospital administrators balked when they realized that putting time and resources into the exchange wasn't part of their own institution's long-range strategic plan. They balked again when they found out the return on their investment couldn't be accurately estimated. They balked a third time over the cost, set at $2 million per hospital. They eventually came up with a strategy that included a smaller price tag, no initial cost to doctors, and a plan to eventually fund the exchange via a small surcharge on lab tests and other services. "We learned from all of this that things don't happen overnight," Edward Koschka, chief information officer of the Community Health Network, says. "There are all sorts of reasons you shouldn't do this, and we had many naysayers in this city. To succeed, you need physicians, CEOs, and CIOs who embrace the vision."[8]

Thornier issues will include:

Changing the culture of health care. In a recent study at Roudebush Veterans Affairs Medical Center in Indiana, researchers found that emergency department doctors routinely wrote orders on paper and handed them off to others to enter into a computer.[9] The doctors said that was more efficient than searching for a computer to enter the orders themselves. Getting busy doctors to tackle the EMR learning curve will be a challenge.

Louise Liang, MD, retired Kaiser Permanente senior vice president, demonstrates in her book, *Connected for Health: Using Electronic Health Records to Transform Care Delivery*, that a comprehensive culture change is necessary before the value of an EHR can be fully realized. One contributor, Medical Director for Operations, Kaiser Permanente-Southern California Dr. Paul Minardi, writes: "In summary, the IT-enabled transformation of an integrated care delivery system is complex, arduous, and filled with unexpected findings. In the end, enhancing our organizational value requires explicit delivery system changes, multiple initiatives, and engaged organizational leadership to execute this change."

But he adds, "Despite those hurdles, we are continually improving on the availability of KP HealthConnect information to support decisions on enhancements to our daily operations, physician proficiency with KP HealthConnect, and analysis of our care delivery patterns."

Convincing doctors that interconnected EHRs are worth their time—and money. In Whatcom County, Washington, a health information network that links 300 doctors let them use the system for free for three years. During that time, doctors' feedback was used to tweak the system for better performance and easier use. Now, doctors pay $71 per month to share medical data and receive lab information online. Only three of the 300 doctors who tried the system for free dropped out once when the bill arrived.[10] What's more, a study by the

National Partnership showed that patients with access to the information in an EHR have greater trust in their physician. Increased patient trust? Priceless.[11]

Giving doctors and care teams a system that is easy to use. In a world where anyone can get elegant access to a world of information by swiping a finger across an iPhone's screen, tolerance for clunky interfaces and lack of integration is minimal. Yet, before consumer tech devices can be put to use in a healthcare setting, they need to be made more robust, secure, and scalable. A device that works fine for a family of five is less likely to hold up in an organization of 5,000 or 50,000. But this can, and is, being done. For example, we've come a long way in improving the user interface for EHRs and EMRs.

Proving to patients that connected systems are private and secure. In a 2012 online survey of 1,061 adults from the National Partnership for Women & Families, 59 percent said their doctors used electronic medical records. But whether their data was stored in a computer or a manila folder, privacy and security were top worries. Fifty-nine percent with electronic files and 66 percent with paper files said they believe widespread adoption of EHR systems will lead to more personal information being lost or stolen. And about 52 percent said they think the privacy of their medical information isn't well protected by federal and state laws or by health institutions[12] Interestingly, a National Partnership study revealed that people with the most concern over the privacy of their EHR had never used one.[13] I would argue that giving people a view into their medical records will help them realize that their EHR is not a mysterious black box, but a tool for them, as well as their caregivers, to use. Equally important in the privacy and security conversation is building a culture of shared responsibility between providers, payers, and patients. In a world where people are posting their latest rash on Facebook or tweeting about their cycling injury, the lines around expected privacy can become blurred.

Health Financial Exchanges

Although these challenges are significant, they are not insurmountable. Laws can be, and, I believe, will be developed to support reform. The industry will respond in kind, but the HIEs will be widely adopted only if they are mandated or if the economic incentive is powerfully aligned to better health outcomes. After all, the industry has a rich history as an unconnected group of individuals paid to provide care. Contributing to health outcomes for community members outside their particular practice was not part of the bargain. So it will take legislation—and a bit of capitalism always helps.

Smart entrepreneurs will see HIEs as a business opportunity. Charging just pennies to measure the quality and accuracy of information and to move information rapidly will be profitable due to the high volumes involved—systems move millions of pieces of information per year. In this way, HIEs could be self-sustaining entities whose existence and cost are funded by a tiny percentage of the money they're saving the system.

We have a model we can look to for how this might work. Fedwire is a system operated by the U.S. Federal Reserve Banks that enables financial institutions to transfer funds electronically between its more than 9,000 participants (as of March 19, 2009). In conjunction with the privately held Clearing House Interbank Payments System (CHIPS), Fedwire is the primary U.S. network for large-value or time-critical domestic and international payments, and it is designed to be highly resilient and redundant. A phenomenal amount of money travels through Fedwire: In June 2012, 11,006,829 transfers accounted for more than $51 million—safely, securely, and efficiently.[14]

The healthcare industry needs its own version of Fedwire. As health reform plays out, we will need an entity that can bear financial risks for the exchange of health information. This new entity will support the concept of primary care as the "hub of care" for each patient—the patient-centered medical home. It would manage an individual's care across all providers, maintain complete health records by aggregating them from HIEs, navigate between specialists, and some believe act as payment agent to specialists and possibly hospitals. Asking primary care doctors to take on this role is asking too much of the physicians on the front lines of basic health care in this country. But a health financial exchange could.

There have been a few attempts to develop the online repository aspect of a health financial exchange: Microsoft's Health Vault, Google Health, Revolution Health, and Aetna's SmartSource (a partnership with Healthline). Microsoft calls Health Vault "a trusted place for people to organize, store, and share health information online." It enables sharing by allowing users to import health records from their doctors, hospitals, labs, prescription drug plans, and other healthcare providers, attempting to take health information out of its silos. Google Health was based "on the idea that with more and better information, people can make smarter choices… in regard to managing personal health and wellness…" The service did not attract as many users as hoped and was discontinued in 2011.[15]

Neither of these services, however, addresses how to monetize and sustain the ongoing exchange of health information. Clearly, there will be a role for financial institutions as we move forward. This may be in the form of an integrated healthcare wallet, similar to the Health Savings Accounts and Health Spending Accounts that exist today. The explosion of mobile payment using smartphones also offers new avenues to explore related to office visit copays made and reflected electronically in one's EHR.

Whereas innovations begin with people in search of a solution, cash has always been the fuel for innovation. Funding is necessary to usher innovations to market and ultimately reach scale. As the approach to health care evolves, so too will financing, for everything from incentive payments for keeping populations healthier than a benchmark, to financing mechanisms that can support the delivery of health IT to small practices. Measuring performance against goals will trump reimbursement based on treatments and office visits. Integrated financial exchanges that enable seamless payment to care providers for better health outcomes will become the oil that moves the machinery, easing administration and drawing a more direct line between incentives and health. We already have a financial system. What we will need in this new era of health is a connected financing system that uses information technology to enable the flow of payment. Many may argue that we already have this system. Banks or insurance companies could fill this role, but necessity will be the mother of invention. The industry must create innovative ways for providers to be paid based on performance and the achievement of defined goals.

Money will flow to new and innovative health financial exchanges that are linked to continuously improving patient outcomes. These exchanges will provide incentive payments to care providers for delivering health outcomes. And the patient wins, because payment is finally aligned with the patient goal of better health. It's so simple. It makes perfect sense. But today, payment and outcomes are not aligned. This switch is as fundamental as breathing is to living. Getting this right is as necessary to the transformation of health care as any medical advance, and any technology.

First, however, we will need significant investments to explore, design, and implement the technologies and systems that will transform the future of health care. The seeds have already been planted in pilot projects and by early adopters. Now we need to scale up and keep up with—or ahead of—the pace of technology in areas like mobility.

HIEs and HFEs Serve the Patient and Create Profit

HIEs will unlock the full potential of electronic medical records. They will allow electronic health data to be transmitted quickly and accurately among doctors, hospitals, emergency rooms, labs, and patients themselves. Now available in certain cities, states, and organizations, we need to create a nationwide network of HIEs.

There are hurdles. Money will be a major factor in getting us there. The seed money provided in the Federal HITECH Act to create regional health IT extension centers is a start. Interoperability is another. We need to ensure that systems made by different manufacturers can connect and communicate easily. A related hurdle is the need for industry-wide standards to ensure that shared data is accurate, up-to-date, accessible, and secure.

While we get HIEs figured out, we also need to work out a business model, something people are starting to call HFEs, or health financial exchanges. As healthcare reform plays out, we will need an entity that can bear financial risks for the exchange of health information. An HFE could function like Fedwire, the system that enables more than 9,000 financial institutions to transfer funds electronically from one to another. This new entity will support the concept of primary care as the hub of care for each patient and could even act as payment agent to specialists and possibly hospitals

Healthcare IT has other lessons to learn from the financial industry, which I will explore in the next chapter, along with a few areas that are ripe for a dose of old-fashioned capitalism and newfangled entrepreneurship.

Notes

1. Susannah Patton, "Sharing Data, Saving Lives," *CIO Magazine*, 2005, www.pageout.net/user/www/j/a/janicelee/Case%20Studies/ Sharing%20Data%20saving%20lives.doc.

2. HITECH Priority Grants Program, www.hhs.gov/recovery/pro- grams/hitech/factsheet.html.

3. HIMSS Stage 7, http://xnet.kp.org/newscenter/pressreleases/nat/2 012/022212stage7himssdavies.html.

4. Katie Coleman, "Implications of Reassigning Patients for the Medical Home: A Case Study," *Annals of Family Medicine* 8, no. 6 (November 2010): 493–498.

5. HIMSS Analytics: Citizens Memorial Healthcare (CMH), www. himssanalytics.org/hc_providers/stage7casestudies_CMH.asp.

6. HIMSS Analytics: Children's Hospital of Pittsburgh of UPMC, www.himssanalytics.org/hc_providers/stage7casestudies_UPMC.asp.

7. Mark L. Wess, "Application of a Decision Support Tool for Anticoagulation in Patients with Nonvalvular Atrial Fibrillation," *Journal of General Internal Medicine* 23, no. 4 (April 2008: 411–417.

8. Patton, "Sharing Data, Saving Lives."

9. J. J. Saleem, "Exploring the Persistence of Paper with the Electronic Health Record," *International Journal of Medical Informatics* 78, no. 9 (September 2009): 618–628. www.ncbi.nlm.nih.gov/pubmed/19464231?dopt=Abstract

10. Patton, "Sharing Data, Saving Lives."

11. National Partnership for Women & Families, *Making IT Meaningful: How Consumers Value and Trust Health IT*, February 2012, www.nationalpartnership.org/site/PageServer?pagename=issues_health_IT_survey.

12. Ibid.

13. Ibid.

14. Federal Reserve Bank Services, June 2012, www.frbservices.org/operations/fedwire/fedwire_funds_services_statistics.html.

15. Google blog post, June 2011, http://googleblog.blogspot.com/2011/06/update-on-google-health-and-google.html#!/2011/06/update-on-google-health-and-google.html.

Chapter 3

Investing in Healthcare IT Innovations

Where the Winners Are

Investors scour the globe for the next big thing—but perhaps they should look no further than the smartphones tucked into their own pockets, purses, and briefcases. As doctors, health insurance companies, and health information companies push more apps and services directly to consumers—and provide more mobile links to electronic health records—investment dollars are already following and fueling an explosion in healthcare information technology. I expect this to be a major growth area in the next decade and beyond. Why?

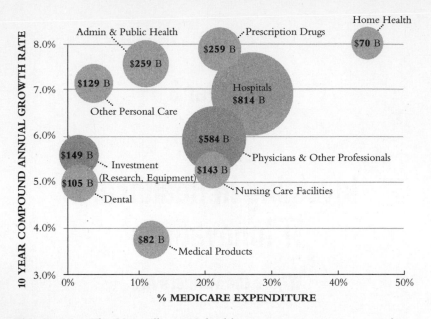

Figure 3.1 The $2.6 trillion U.S. healthcare system is as unconnected as it is costly. Indeed, it is costly in part because it is unconnected.
SOURCE: Kaiser Permanente.

Having a healthcare system that spends $2.6 trillion annually is distressing enough. What makes the situation even more dire is how much of that cost is related to the lack of connection among the various parts of the system. (See Figure 3.1) Better alignment would cut costs while delivering more integrated, coordinated care. (See Figure 3.2)

- Market research indicates spending on healthcare IT (HIT) and on connecting these systems will grow at an even faster rate than overall healthcare spending. According to the company Insight Research, healthcare IT spending will grow 9.7 percent annually between 2012 and 2017. That compares to an annual 6.4 percent growth rate in overall healthcare spending over the same

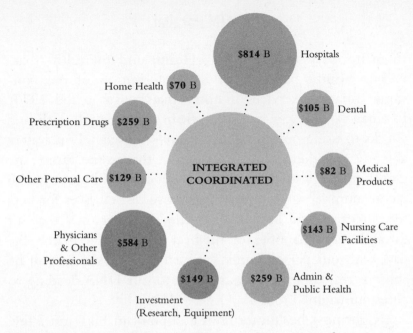

Figure 3.2 A connected system of integrated care, using information technology, will help us achieve better health outcomes, make the system more efficient, save resources, and create opportunities for innovation. SOURCE: Kaiser Permanente.

period of time. In dollars, that pencils out to an increase from $9.1 billion to $14.4 billion over five years.[1]

- As more and more healthcare providers go digital, link records via health information exchanges (HIEs), and gear up to meet the federal government's meaningful use criteria, the respected market research firm Black Book Rankings predicts HIT and HIE spending will triple.[2]

- Top HIT vendors agree. Neal Patterson, founder and CEO of Cerner, the largest stand-alone developer of healthcare IT systems on the planet, told *Forbes* magazine in May 2012 that he expects HIT sales in the United States to double or even quadruple by 2020. That means the market could grow from $5 billion to $10 billion annually.[3]

The ATM Parallel

In many ways, the move to eHealth and mHealth (that's mobile health) parallels the computerization of the consumer financial services industry that began in the 1970s. In financial services, we went from paying with cash and checks to using our credit card numbers—securely, privately, anytime, anywhere. Similarly, I expect that in the future, the global currency used for medical services will be our health record number. Our ability to improve our chances for better outcomes will be fueled by thinking machines that sift through vast quantities of medical science and match the data with our personal medical histories. Physicians will be able to treat us with drugs specific to our DNA, leading to cures unimagined today.

Right now, healthcare IT is at a point in HIT just a few paces beyond where the financial services industry found itself in 1969, when the first automated teller machine in the United States dispensed its first $20 bill outside Chemical Bank in Rockville Centre, New York. It opened for business just six weeks after the United States landed the first men on the moon.[4] Are we on the cusp of another giant leap for mankind as American health care connects its resources? I believe the answer is a firm yes.

IT systems revolutionized financial services in many ways. Banks saved money as consumers used ATMs for deposits and withdrawals, and ultimately made purchases and paid their bills online. According to a Bain & Company brief, transaction costs have dropped from $4 at the teller window to just 8 cents when you pay a bill using your smartphone.[5] Not to mention the convenience of 24/7 access to your accounts.

The financial services industry's willingness to invest in technology fueled other innovations like online trading, expanded financial-management capabilities for consumers, and the rise of accurate, real-time data from the world's financial markets.[6] And the digital push led the financial services industry to increase investment in IT from 3 percent of revenue in the early 1990s to 10 percent by the end of the decade. Today, IT spending uses about 6 to 8 percent of the industry's revenues. This compares to a mere 3 percent of revenue in the healthcare sector. Is it enough? Maybe not—and the numbers cited at the start of this chapter suggest that healthcare leaders are aware and poised to accelerate investment.[7]

The healthcare industry is on the cusp of significant change. As our knowledge is expanded by systems and analytics providing more and deeper insights, we'll reap healthier customers, lower costs, and faster medical breakthroughs.

Consumers: Ahead of the Curve

I hear the same questions over and over again in discussions of healthcare IT: Do consumers want it? Do they see the value? Do they trust it?

The financial services industry had the same questions. A look at how consumers have responded to IT innovations in that sphere provides clues to their readiness for healthcare IT.

Do consumers want it? As recently as 2000, most bank customers would have given you a blank stare if you asked whether they wanted to bank online using their computers. Yet, banks had been offering some computerized services back in the 1980s. In 1995, Wells Fargo Bank broke new ground when it became the first American bank to offer online account services via its website.[8] Today, 4 in 5 U.S. households—that's at least 72 million households—with Internet access their bank online. As Robert DeYoung, then an associate director in the Division of Insurance and Research at the Federal Deposit Insurance Corporation noted in a 2007 paper, "Internet banking has changed the landscape of the financial services industry by reducing both the importance of geography and the cost of transactions."

One of the biggest and most convenient changes came when banks offered the ability to pay bills online, which DeYoung calls "possibly the biggest impact of technology on the banking system."[9] According to ongoing Federal Reserve payment studies, paper checks went from being the dominant noncash form of payments in 2001 to being used less than 20 percent of the time in 2010.[10]

Over 36 million people paid bills online in 2010, up 10 percent over the year before, and the numbers have only continued to grow.[11] It's not just Generation X, either. Online bill-paying is mainstream, with large percentages of all age groups—young adults, those in midlife, and those over age 55—clicking to take care of finances rather than writing checks or reaching into their wallets.[12] And it is instructive to note that women, who are also so often the healthcare "chief information officers" for their families, are more likely than men to be a family's primary online bill-payer.[13]

I predict something similar will happen with health care. As systems go digital and connect, an ID number will replace your insurance card, and you will schedule appointments, make payments, and track your care and your healthcare finances online. No more need to hold on to all that paper from your insurance company or keep track of paper bills from your doctor!

Do consumers see the value? You need look no further than the credit cards in your wallet. Early on—we're talking the 1920s—gas stations, department stores, and hotel chains offered their own credit cards to customers as a convenience.

By the 1950s, wider-use cards like Diners Club, American Express, and Bank of America became available. Going digital in the 1970s and 1980s allowed banks and companies of all sorts to improve their analysis of consumer purchasing data. The result is the personalized offers and the anytime, anywhere convenient access we enjoy today.[14]

Do they trust it? Concerns over the security and privacy of their financial records may have caused some banking customers to hesitate in the early days. Today, most consumers are comfortable with the precautions the banking industry has put in place.

This is clearly a major issue for healthcare IT. Unless consumers are comfortable with the security and confidentiality of their information and the systems, they will not be comfortable using them. Secure, private systems are an absolute necessity, no ifs, ands, or buts. The healthcare industry has already developed standards for interconnected electronic health records, proof of how seriously we take those concerns and of our commitment to delivering workable, secure solutions.

Up Next: Mobile Banking *and* Mobile Health

Healthcare has the opportunity and challenge to jump into the mobile arena at the same time the financial services industry leaps in. In many ways, this realm of mobility is leading the charge, as doctors and consumers alike use tablets and smartphones even if they don't have fully-functioning EHR systems, and even if those systems still exist in silos, disconnected from any larger network. The March 2012 Federal Reserve report "Consumers and Mobile Financial Services" found that one in five consumers with mobile phones and a bank account were already using mobile banking.[15]

In the future, consumers will use mobile devices to manage their finances and their health in similar ways. They'll pull info from many sources when shopping for a mortgage, a credit card, a home equity loan to build a new deck, or a nursery for a new baby. Apps will connect people to a huge variety of data.

Cloud computing—shifting applications and data from local computers to a more efficient network of computers in a data center anywhere in the world—will over time emerge as an important component of affordable EHR systems and nimble information exchanges. As this new technology becomes more pervasive and secure, it will reshape the cost of entry, further accelerating new trends. And it will substantially broaden the use and adoption of health IT tools.

If you have any doubts about the future of mobile technology, here's an eye-opening statistic: In 2010, more smartphones were purchased worldwide than personal computers, with over 100 million new smartphones bought by consumers around the world.[16] The future is here. And in health care, as in consumer financial services, it's mobile, it's connected, it's personal, it's powerful—and it's 24/7.

Investing in Winning Healthcare IT Innovation

We've moved beyond early adopters of EHR systems and "model" HIEs. In the trenches, winning EHR systems and HIEs must meet the needs of providers and payers who expect a real return on investment by way of systems that meet real needs. Although some 1,300 vendors offer or have offered EHRs to physicians and medical centers, that doesn't mean this healthcare IT building block is finished as an avenue for innovation and investment. Though there are many choices among these systems, this is still the first generation of tools. As with all technology, innovation occurs, then improvements, then more innovation. Thus far, EHRs are built for large-scale computers like mainframes. Over time they will increasingly operate in the cloud or as building blocks assembled on demand, forming an ecosystem dedicated to supporting consumers' evolving health needs. Like many industries affected by technology, health care will see the rise of the consumer as a force that demands new capabilities, convenience, and tools. Frankly, the winners will be those organizations who create consumer-centric tool kits that are intuitive, easy to use, and mobile.

Meanwhile, HIEs are claiming more attention and dollars—putting interoperability on the cutting edge. The enterprise HIE vendor marketplace is in flux as new start-ups compete with established systems and traditional tech firms move in to the healthcare space. All of them are intent on "attempting to capture the escalating spend for true interoperability," as Black Book rightly described it in the spring of 2012. There's real opportunity here. According to Black Book's 2012 *State of the Health Information Exchange Industry* report, 80 percent of U.S. hospitals and 97 percent of American doctors were not interconnected in the first quarter of 2012. But the firm's survey of 4,000 healthcare delivery and insurance organizations found that 84 percent are actively working to adopt HIE.[17]

At the same time, there's plenty of growth ahead for a wide variety of mobile-health applications, for analytics capable of slicing and dicing giant data sets to find life-saving and cost-saving patterns in health care, for more sophisticated telemedicine, and for a dizzying array of solutions for all the little needs that crop up when existing systems go digital and need to talk to each other and simply function day to day. (Case in point: protective covers for physicians' tablets and other mobile devices that are impervious to fluids and to the inevitable drops that happen in a hospital or medical office.)

There will be huge opportunities for the technology industry, inventors, and entrepreneurial minds across all sectors in the area of analysis and virtual capabilities. Analytics of all kinds will be needed to make sense of all the data. When online banking was untilled ground in the financial industry, firms like SAS prospered, as its bevy of mathematicians made analysis simpler and data more accessible.

The same will happen in the healthcare industry. Many discoveries will come from this yet unanalyzed data. Virtual capabilities that assemble data into information on demand will be key to the consumerization of technology. Applets will emerge that consumers will use on their smartphones and couple with their medical record number to find all sorts of new services customized to their individual situations. Everything from health information to health coaches in the form of mobile apps are already at our fingertips and will just become more robust, making health care as accessible as booking a table for dinner or checking your bank account balance.

Here's the latest from the leading edge of HIT in four important areas:

#1: Cloud Computing Gets Past the Pain Point of Cost

In 2011, 55 percent of doctors had at least some basic EMR systems, and of those, 75 percent met government standards for meaningful use, according to the Centers for Disease Control and Prevention.[18] Granted, those numbers are changing almost daily as more and more get on board. But we're beyond the tech-savvy early adopters. Physicians and medical centers who aren't yet digital are looking for simple, affordable, seamless systems that can go live without taking enormous amounts of time away from patient care.

Getting adopters past what one Robert Wood Johnson Foundation report called the "adoption pain point of cost"[19] will take creativity and an understanding of what healthcare providers really need. But investing in innovative health IT is a winning strategy for entrepreneurs. Good systems (Epic, Cerner, and others) have turned the people who founded and run top EHR companies into what *Forbes* magazine called "Obamacare Billionaires."[20]

What's next? Cloud computing is one disruptive technology that makes setting up and running an EHR faster, simpler, and more affordable. Examples include eClinicalWorks and Athena Health.[21] Bain and Company suggests that the move to cloud computing could cut costs 30 to 40 percent compared to legacy IT systems.[22] That is a big selling point. The smartest new EHR vendors go the extra mile to guarantee, as Athena Health does, that the systems they deliver will allow a practice to qualify for Medicare Meaningful Use payments. That's a step beyond promising that a system is merely "certified" for Meaningful Use. This is a smart strategy for vendors, as it gives healthcare providers an income stream that will help defray the cost of adopting the technology.

As Athena Health promises, "As Meaningful Use progresses through Stages 2 and 3, our clients know we'll be staying on top of requirements and helping ensure that they stay compliant and receive all available incentives . . . [it's] never a question of whether; just a question of when."[23]

#2: Analytics for Big Data Sets

Here at Kaiser Permanente, the one to two terabytes of data we've collected each day since 2003 have created a patient database that's bigger than the Library of Congress. Our system can analyze and leverage this massive data set with a variety of tools: Predictive analytics, clinical decision support, data mining, and natural language processing are among them. What we have learned has changed the way we, and doctors around the world, practice medicine.

For example, an analysis of a Kaiser Permanente database of 1.4 million members led to the discovery that the COX-2 pain reliever Vioxx, widely used by arthritis patients, was dangerous.[24] Ultimately, the drug was taken off the market. It took a big data set and the right tools to find this life-saving information. Future data sets will rely on even deeper knowledge of human health, incorporating genomics, digital pathology reports, and new types of imaging.

Big data is also making a difference at the Lee Moffitt Cancer Center & Research Institute in Tampa, Florida, where a personalized research program called Total Cancer Care delivers day-to-day benefits for cancer patients and long-term benefits for the rest of us. The system, supported by Oracle, tracks cancer patients during treatment and for the rest of their lives. All levels of data are kept: clinical data, genetics, treatment outcomes, and samples of blood, urine, and tumor tissue from surgeries and biopsies. The goal is to determine which treatment options work best for individual patients, expanding what we know for certain about individualized, targeted cancer care with the aim of achieving higher survival rates in the future.

Started in 2003, Total Cancer Care "addresses cancer as a public health issue and takes a holistic approach by encompassing all aspects of the disease, including preventive measures such as the study of genetic predispositions, impact of health lifestyles and integrative medicine. Total Cancer Care follows the patient throughout her or his life, including screening, diagnosis and treatment of cancer. Translational research is incorporated at each step along this continuum of care and follow-up," according to the center.[25]

The beauty is that the program collects data with no extra patient visits. It simply takes full advantage of data collected during a patient's care. It's up to patients to sign up, and the incentive is strong. As the center says, "Someday, you or others participating in this research may need drug therapy to treat your disease. Should this occur, we would want to use gene-based technology to try to find the best drug for you."

Big data is another huge opportunity for innovators and investors, one that has already attracted the attention of major players like Dell, Intel, and Oracle. Storage alone is a challenge. Research shows that providers now dump nearly 90 percent of data (such as video feeds from surgery) due to storage issues—literally tossing into the garbage information that could save lives. Analytics could become a $10-billion market by 2020.

This will also create a pool of jobs in search of talent. By 2018, the United States may not have enough workers with deep analytical skills, predicts the McKinsey Global Institute in its 2011 report, *Big Data: The Next Frontier for Innovation, Competition, and Productivity*. The shortage may be as big as 190,000 analysts with advanced abilities and 1.5 million managers and others who understand how to put the results to good use.[26]

#3: Telehealth Is Mobile Health, Too

Beyond the health potential of mobile devices, other wireless breakthroughs are improving home care for the elderly, people with chronic conditions, and anyone recovering from surgery or other medical care. This is another important growth area, as hospitals strive to lower costs by sending patients home on time and ensuring that their recovery goes well, lowering readmission rates. The best way to do that is with care that follows you home from the hospital.

Enter the new world of telemedicine (the delivery of care via telecommunication technologies like video) and telehealth (beyond care, telehealth includes preventive health services, such as medical education and e-mail consultation). It's all about high-tech tracking and high-touch connection. According to BCC Research, telehome technologies were a $3.5 billion global market in 2011, and are expected to reach $9.7 billion in 2016.[27]

Innovations include portable pulse oximeters that can send data on pulse and blood oxygen rates from a patient sitting at home to his doctor, in real time, via Honeywell HomMed's LifeStream platform.[28] Health buddy systems will help you stick with your exercise routine or new stop-smoking plan, while interactive systems allow you to send info about your daily health—blood sugar, blood pressure, fatigue level, weight, and more—to your doctor for immediate evaluation.

On a larger scale, a cloud-based telehealth service provider called ConsultADoctor is up and running, with a network of U.S. board-certified physicians in all 50 states who provide on-demand services like e-prescriptions, e-medical records, and e-lab testing to hospitals, clinics, and integrated health systems.[29]

Though this area is just emerging, its potential is clear. It could well go beyond a physician checking in with you every few minutes to include apps that monitor your vitals continuously, interpreting your health status for you and your clinical team. Intervention and support will be just a click or a swipe away. It's your choice.

#4: Detail-Oriented Innovations

Can your doctor's iPhone withstand a splash of disinfectant? Can the dozens of vital-sign monitors in your local emergency room send their data to your EHR? Can your pillbox alert your doctor when you skip your medication? Not all healthcare IT innovations have to be sophisticated high-tech solutions. Medical start-ups that know how to tie up all the loose ends are big business, and will continue to be.

Often, these technologies start in the consumer goods sector and are translated into a healthcare setting. But that translation requires making sure that the solutions used in healthcare settings are robust, secure, and comply with often stringent regulations. We will need entrepreneurial companies of all sizes that can move solutions from the consumer market into the healthcare markets.

Take gaming systems, for example. There are signs that technology borrowed from the Xbox your kids love will someday enable practitioners to page through medical records and images in the operating room using motion sensors alone, without ever touching a key or a screen. In Spain, Kinect technology was recently tested in an operating room, where doctors navigated MRIs and CAT scans with a wave of the hand.[30]

Voice-enabled apps were the focus of the Nuance 2012 Mobile Clinician Voice Challenge. The winner: Montrue Technologies' Sparrow EDIS application, developed on Nuance's 360 Development platform. Sparrow EDIS allows healthcare software vendors to embed speech recognition into clinical workflow applications. In particular, it incorporates Speech Anywhere, a cloud-based tool that developers employ to speech-enable mobile apps.[31]

Detail-oriented innovations crop up everywhere. How about one that helps doctors remember to fill in overlooked sections of a patient's EHR? New software from Nuance, called the Dragon Medical 360 M.D. Assist, pinpoints missing data fast.[32] Developed with 3M Health Information Systems, it can prompt doctors for information necessary to comply with new coding standards.

Want to check in via tablet at your next doctor's appointment? Software enabling that will be incorporated into new Motorola tablets. Hospitals and medical centers are reaping the benefits from systems that integrate vital-sign monitors with hospital information systems. There's even digital technology for counting sponges in surgery, so none are left behind. And let's not overlook bar coding. Yes, it's already on everything you buy, from jeans to milk to toothpaste. But bar codes on medications, proven to slash medical errors, are still not the norm in most U.S. hospitals. Another digital need looking for a solution: A bar code printer that ties in wirelessly to the institution's information systems.

Looking for Investment in All the Right Places

Innovation takes investment as well as ideas. It may be in the form of capital expense, venture or angel capital, bank loans, credit cards, or borrowing from friends and family. One new and promising financial resource is accelerator programs for entrepreneurs. Two of them, Rock Health, founded in San Francisco, and Healthbox, in Chicago, focus on healthcare innovation.

In August 2012, Healthbox announced the 10 participants in its first three-month accelerator program for entrepreneurs working on new products and services for the healthcare industry. Participants get free office space, mentorship, and $50,000 in seed funding in return for a seven percent equity stake. Their projects demonstrate the scope of innovative solutions the healthcare industry is clamoring for: a "cap" for asthma inhalers that monitors usage and sends data to the patient's care team, and software to help physicians explain specific medical conditions to patients and that presents lab results in an easy-to-understand, intuitive format.

Opportunities for Innovation and Return on Investment Abound

Market researchers and companies already involved in the sector agree: Spending on health IT will explode in the next 5 to 10 years. We need look no further than the familiar ATM machine to see how quickly consumers will adopt new technology if it is convenient, easy to use, and secure. Now, it is time for hospitals and physicians to catch up with their patients. The day is coming when consumers will use their mobile devices to manage their health as they now use them to manage their finances.

There will be growth opportunities not just in the big systems—EMRs, HIEs, and HFEs (health financial exchanges)—but in smaller innovations as well. Cloud computing, data analysis, and mobile applications all offer room for growth. And sometimes, innovation can be the "next little thing." Paying attention to details like a smartphone case that can survive a splash of disinfectant or a pillbox that requests prescription refills automatically can pay off in profits and better health outcomes.

In fact, smartphones will play a big role in transforming health care. Mobile devices mean that any place can be the right place to deliver healthcare information. Mobile technology has already changed how we connect with families and work, with our finances and friends. It is about to change our relationships with our physicians and personal health information as well.

Notes

1. The Insight Research Corporation, "Telecom, IT and Healthcare: Wireless Networks, Digital Healthcare and the Transformation of US Healthcare, 2012–2017," http://insight-corp.com/reports/tele-health12.asp.

2. "Healthcare IT Spending to Grow by Triple Digits: Black Book HIE Survey," www.prweb.com/releases/2012/5/prweb9550653.htm.

3. Matthew Herper, "Obamacare Billionaire: What One Entrepreneur's Rise Says about the Future of Medicine," *Forbes*, April 18, 2012, www.forbes.com/sites/matthewherper/2012/04/18/obamacare-billionaire-what-one-entrepreneurs-rise-says-about-the-future-of-medicine/print/.

4. "This Day in Tech: Events That Shaped the Wired World: Sept. 2, 1969: First U.S. ATM Starts Doling Out Dollars," Kim Zetter, *Wired*, September 2, 2010, www.wired.com/thisdayintech/2010/09/0902first-us-atm/.

5. Chuck Farkas and Tim van Biesen, Bain Brief: "The Future of Healthcare—There's an App for That," June 5, 2012, www.bain.com/publications/articles/the-future-of-healthcare.aspx.

6. Ibid.

7. Ibid.

8. Wells Fargo, "Wells Fargo Marks 15 Years of Serving Customers Online: Pioneering Spirit Led Wells Fargo to Become First Bank in the Nation to Enable Customers 'Anytime, Anywhere' Access to Accounts," May 18, 2010, https://www.wellsfargo.com/press/2010/20100518_OnlineBanking.

9. Robert DeYoung, "Safety, Soundness, and the Evolution of the U.S. Banking Industry," *Economic Review*, First and Second Quarters

2007, Federal Deposit Insurance Corporation, www.frbatlanta.org/filelegacydocs/erq107_DeYoung.pdf.

10. Federal Reserve Financial Services, "Journey through the Payments Study: Check Changes through the Decade," *FedFocus*, www.frbservices.org/fedfocus/archive_general/general_0311_01.html.

11. Andrea McKenna, "More Consumers Embracing Online Banking, Bill Pay," *American Banker*, June 2010, www.americanbanker.com/bulletins/-1020520-1.html?zkPrintable=true.

12. Ibid.

13. Ibid.

14. M. J. Stephey, "A Brief History of Credit Cards," *Time*, April 23, 2009, www.time.com/time/magazine/article/0,9171,1893507,00.html#ixzz1yBQeK7yI.

15. Federal Reserve, "Consumers and Mobile Financial Services," March 2012, www.federalreserve.gov/econresdata/mobile-device-report-201203.pdf.

16. Steve King and Carolyn Ockels, Intuit 2020 Report: *The Future of Financial Services*, April 11, 2011, www.banking2020.com/2011/04/11/intuit-2020-report-the-future-of-the-financial-services-industry/ .

17. Black Book 2012, "State of the Health Information Exchange Industry," www.blackbookrankings.com/healthcare/rankings-health-information-exchange.php, reported in *Healthcare IT News*, "Health IT Spending Flying High, Survey Says," May 31, 2012, www.healthcareitnews.com/news/health-it-spending-flying-high-survey-says.

18. Eric Jamoom, Paul Beatty, Anita Bercovitz, David Woodwell, Kathleen Palso, and Elizabeth Rechtsteiner, "Physician Adoption of Electronic Health Record Systems: United States, 2011," NCHS Data Brief no. 98, July 2012, U.S. Department of Health and Human Services, Centers for Disease Control and Prevention, National Center for Health Statistics, . www.cdc.gov/nchs/data/databriefs/db98.pdf.

19. "Health Information Technology in the United States: Driving toward Delivery System Change, 2012," Robert Wood Johnson Foundation, www.rwjf.org/files/research/74262.5822.hit.full.rpt.final.041612.pdf.

20. Herper, "Obamacare Billionaire."

21. Cloud, Practice Fusion www.practicefusion.com/.

22. Farkas and van Biesen, "The Future of Healthcare."

23. Athena Health promise, www.athenahealth.com/meaningful-use.php#/IntroMU.

24. D. J. Graham, "Risk of Acute Myocardial Infarction and Sudden Cardiac Death in Patients Treated with Cyclo-Oxygenase 2 Selective and Non-Selective Non-Steroidal Anti-Inflammatory Drugs: Nested Case-Control Study," *Lancet* 365 (2005): 475-481, http://www.biomedcentral.com/content/pdf/ar2047.pdf.

25. Lee Moffitt Cancer Center & Research Institute: Total Cancer Care, http://www.moffitt.org/totalcancercare.

26. James Manyika, "Big Data: The Next Frontier for Innovation, Competition, and Productivity," McKinsey Global Institute, May 2011, http://www.mckinsey.com/insights/mgi/research/technology_and_innovation/big_data_the_next_frontier_for_inno-vation.

27. BCC Research, "Global Markets for Telemedicine Technologies," http://www.bccresearch.com/report/telemedicine-technologies-global-markets-hlc014e.html.

28. Honeywell HomMed LifeStream™ Platform, http://hommed.com/Products/LifeStream_platform.asp.

29. ConsultADoctor, http://www.consultadr.com/.

30. Xbox, "The Kinect Effect: How The World is Using Kinect," http://www.xbox.com/en-US/Kinect/Kinect-Effect.

31. Nuance Press Release, "Live from HIMSS: Nuance Healthcare Announces Winners of the 2012 Mobile Clinician Voice Challenge," February 22, 2012, http://www.nuance.com/company/news-room/press-releases/HIMSS-2012-Mobile-App-Challenge-2.22-Rls-FINAL_web.doc

32. Dragon Medical 360 M.D., http://www.nuance.com/for-health-care/by-solutions/dragon-medical-360-md-assist/index.htm.

Chapter 4

Virtual Visits

Care Anywhere and Care Everywhere

B ack in the 1950s, no one carried a computer around. How could they? Computers often occupied entire rooms. In the 1980s, they moved onto our desktops, then our laps, and now they fit in the palms of our hands. Similarly, few people would carry around copies of their paper medical files, much less pass them around for their pharmacists or physical therapists to annotate. But this actually still happens today, although with decreasing frequency.

Soon, thanks to a connected system of electronic medical records (EMRs), people will have secure access to their own personal health information, and their caregivers will be able to track patients' vital signs to identify and address health problems before they start. Electronic health records' wireless wellness must do the same thing by taking wireless wellness to the next level: digital health and mobile health.

We're not so far away. Nearly everyone in America carries a cell phone, and many are Internet-linked smartphones. Most of us have computers with Internet access, too. We use these tools every hour of every day to share information—from grocery lists and announcements for the next neighborhood barbecue to high school reunion photos and the latest project at work. It's how we manage our credit cards, pay traffic tickets, even track the office fantasy football league.

Today, 80 percent of U.S. doctors use smartphones and medical apps one way or another in their daily practice of medicine. According to a CompTIA study, nearly one-third of providers use mobile devices (tablet computers, laptops, and smartphones) to access an EHR. Thirty percent of practicing physicians have already purchased an iPad, and another 28 percent plan to do so within the next six months.[1]

Yet when it comes to health, most of us use the Web as if it were an old-fashioned encyclopedia or the yellow pages: We look up symptoms, download first-aid instructions, locate doctors. That's important info, but it's a little like keeping a well-tuned Porsche in the garage just for trips to your mailbox!

Advocates of digital and mobile health say they will increase efficiency and could save billions of dollars. Usually missing from the conversation, though, are specific examples of how these advances improve the lives and well-being of real people. At full throttle, here's how real-time digital health could change your life (Figure 4.1):

- **Lose weight with your cell phone**. Keeping a food diary is a proven way to increase your chances for successful weight loss. Using your cell phone may be even

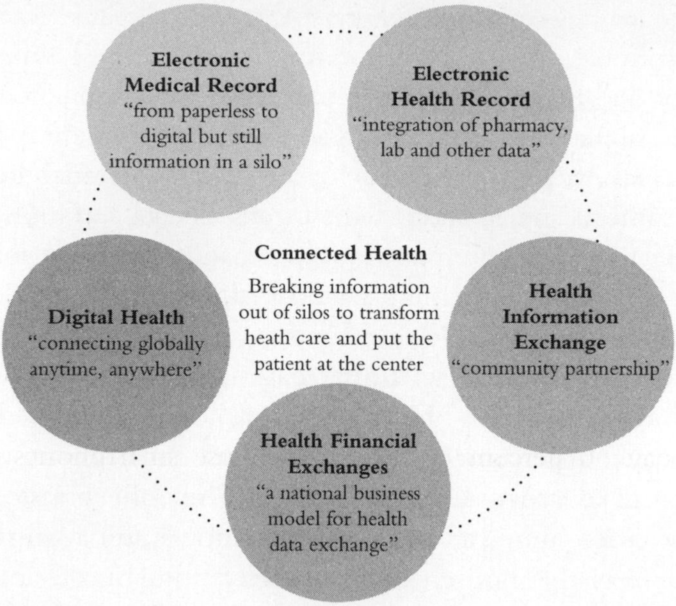

Figure 4.1 Connected health puts the patient in the center of the action.
SOURCE: Kaiser Permanente.

better. The proof? When 43 women and men agreed to photograph every morsel they popped into their mouths for one week, the results, say researchers at the University of Wisconsin-Madison, were eye-opening—and diet-changing. These mealtime paparazzi, who considered themselves healthy eaters before the study, discovered that their portions were too big, they weren't eating enough fruit and vegetables, and their snack choices were downright embarrassing. Simply taking photos nudged some to make healthier choices—one volunteer grabbed a pack of M&Ms, then decided against them when she realized she'd have to photograph them before munching.[2]

Plenty of cell phone apps can help you track calories. The next wave? We're beginning to see services that let you send pictures of your meals to a trained dietitian for fast nutritional analysis. And, for instant analysis and support, apps like Fooducate provide just what the doctor ordered. This application essentially grades the food you are eating. You take a picture of a bar code using the phone's built-in camera. The application then scans its data and immediately provides more nutrition information than you might see even on the label, along with a letter grade. As one colleague said to me, "No one wants to eat D-list food."

- **See your doctor without leaving home**. In Hawaii, a Blue Cross Blue Shield affiliate called Hawaii Medical Service Association offers online and phone visits with on-call doctors. Ten minutes costs members just $10 (the price jumps to $45 for nonmembers, still a bargain). These virtual house calls are great way to handle minor emergencies and some routine care quickly, conveniently, and affordably—in real time.

  It's a lot like the "chat now" feature on many shopping websites. One public health nurse in Hawaii tried it for an infected cut that needed prompt attention. She logged on, chose an available doctor, and clicked "Connect Now." After an online chat, the doctor e-mailed a prescription for an antibiotic to a nearby pharmacy, which she picked up soon after logging off. "Pretty painless," says the nurse, Donita Gano, 59.[3]

  Inexpensive, convenient, and patient friendly, virtual doctor-visit services are springing up across the nation—from Hawaii to Minnesota to New York City. Two services, MDLiveCare and Online Care, are rolling out coast-to-coast programs. On-call docs say they've treated everything from infected cuts to fungal infections to, yes, hemorrhoids. (We'd rather not see the webcam replay of that one!)

- **Check your blood pressure, anywhere and anytime, and then automatically send the numbers to your**

doctor. In a joint pilot study with the Cleveland Clinic and Microsoft's Health Vault (a digital health-monitoring program), 30 people with high blood pressure tested—and loved—a new kind of digital blood-pressure system. They used home blood pressure monitors that automatically uploaded the results to their own online health records and then e-mailed the doctor at the first hint of an irregularity.

This early-warning system lets your doctor adjust medications in real time and see the results, rather than waiting months until your next office visit. One volunteer, a cross-country trucker, had struggled with less-than-stellar blood pressure levels for years. He used the digital tracking system on the road, allowing doctors to spot and fix afternoon blood pressure spikes. His levels are now a very healthy 120/82.[4]

- **Get a better night's sleep**. Millions of Americans struggle with sleep apnea—night-time breathing disruptions that make blood-oxygen levels plummet. The fallout goes beyond fatigue. Apnea raises risk for everything from nodding off at the wheel of your car to weight gain, type 2 diabetes, and high blood pressure. The gold-standard fix is a CPAP—a mask and machine that boosts air pressure when you inhale. They work, but many people find the masks uncomfortable or have trouble adjusting air pressure levels for optimal results. Now, several companies are developing wireless CPAP monitors that tell your doctor whether you're keeping the mask on at night and what the pressure settings are—info that can help you finally get a good night's sleep.[5]

- **Know that an aging parent with dementia is safe at home**. In the United Kingdom, "smart homes" equipped with special sensors are helping older people with dementia live longer at home—safely. Developed by the Bath Institute of Medical Engineering, the sensors can turn off a forgotten burner on the stove, urge a wanderer to return to bed at night if they open the front door (and call for help if they don't), and remind a forgetful occupant to turn off the lights at night or shut off a faucet at the kitchen sink.[6]

- **Got a smartphone? Get connected to health**. At Kaiser Permanente, our website, optimized for mobile devices, plus iPhone and Android applications, give our nine million members convenient and secure access to their own medical information, e-mail their doctors, and order prescriptions from anywhere in the world. Because no data is ever actually stored on the device itself, the information is both totally portable and secure. Other, more targeted tools include the Kaiser Permanente Locator app for finding our facilities and Every Body Walk!, an app that encourages people to maintain healthy activity levels.

Easier Than Programming Your TV Remote Control

Digital health isn't a substitute for superior hands-on care; instead, it gives you and your doctor a higher level of information about your health so that you can both make better-informed decisions. Technology alone will not change health care. But technology coupled with expert physicians and coordinated care teams can ensure you get the ongoing care and attention we all deserve. It's also not intended to diagnose serious, new problems without a real office visit. But it could free you and your doctor so that you need fewer visits to review or check info that can be monitored at home.

What makes digital health tick? Super-easy technology. Some wireless wellness solutions will use equipment you already own, including your cell phone, computer, a web camera, and even your television. At Kaiser Permanente, for example, we've implemented video conferencing technology for high-definition TV that delivers a diagnostic-quality image of a skin rash or troubling bump to your dermatologist. In many cases that's all that is needed for a diagnosis and ultimately treatment.

Digital health also means invisible technology—sending and receiving units built into blood sugar meters and heart devices, or a digital bathroom scale that sends your weight directly to your EHR, for example.

At Kaiser Permanente, we're testing home health equipment that fits on a bookshelf and virtually runs itself. Just press "on" and follow the directions. One machine under development at our Sidney R. Garfield Health Care Innovation Center instructs you on how to use a blood pressure cuff, then asks whether you've taken your medications today and even probes for signs of depression. With Honeywell International, we're testing a clock-radio-sized device that helps people with congestive heart failure track vital signs including weight and blood pressure. Data are sent automatically to the doctor. If weight is up—a sign of dangerous fluid retention—a nurse calls with advice to take more diuretics, for example. Overall, close monitoring has meant fewer hospital visits and more stable heart health for many of the 600 people who've tried it.

When I think about digital health I see convenience, accuracy, and better care (Figure 4.2). Others will see privacy lost and security compromised. Clearly, privacy and security are very significant topics. You need only read the headlines—from the *News of the World* phone hacking scandal in England and incursions into LinkedIn's password database—to understand that people expect a high degree of security

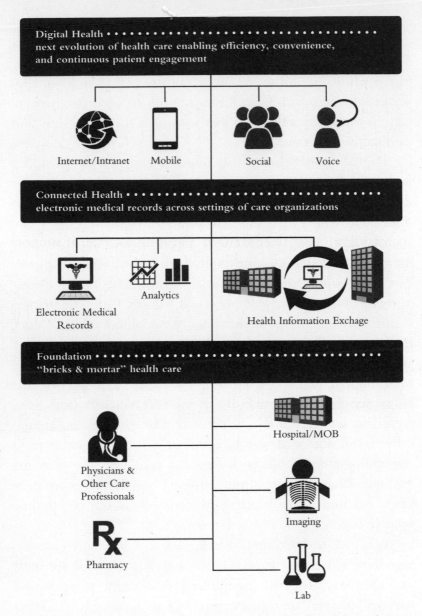

Figure 4.2 Digital health represents a convergence of capabilities that empower consumers to manage their health on their own terms, further redefining the patient-caregiver relationship.

SOURCE: Kaiser Permanente.

and confidentiality. So do we. For one thing, the health-care industry works under strict regulations that hold us to high standards for protecting all patient health information. For another, we know just how valuable and important that data is to our patients and to us. The ability to secure patient information wherever it is accessed, from a hospital system or the patient's mobile phone, will require advances to security technology so we can be assured these innovations are beneficial, not problematic. Maintaining robust controls for EHR and EMR systems is a primary concern. This includes restricting access, controlling where and how data flows, and maintaining network separation. Creating a circle of support around each patient and providing accessible, affordable, anytime care that's secure *can* be done.

The good news? We don't have to wait for a technological breakthrough to get started. If you've had even the briefest encounter with the Internet, or text-messaging, or Facebook, you're familiar with the technologies that will drive this new world. What will have to change: How they're used and how soon consumers and medical professionals adopt them.

I think we're ready. Consider the parents of kids with diabetes, clamoring for the Diabetes Phone so their children get better care. And consider this: One of the newest top-selling categories of smartphone apps are health trackers—dozens of them—designed to help you stay on top of everything from the calories you're eating to how far you jogged to your fertility.

Meanwhile, companies in the technology business are doing a victory lap about now, because we need their services. Dozens are developing home health monitoring equipment as I write this, with the knowledge that everyone in the IT industry wins when home health becomes a reality. It may take a bit longer than some optimists think.

This is truly a marathon. And these emerging companies are just the beginning of a significant wave—a wave of invention that will ultimately benefit everyone, healthy and those with chronic conditions alike. After all, we all want to be in better health. And even if all of us don't, our health care system needs us to be in better health. Technology may be the bridge we need.

Are we truly ready? The answer may depend on who you are. Early adopters of EMRs will adopt and deploy rapidly, making these capabilities available to people sooner. My sense is that the home health revolution will not be a sweeping, breakthrough change—but rather something gradual with the EMR underpinning it all. I expect widespread adoption will occur in about 15 to 20 years, when my oldest children are in their forties. Why so long? Aside from further EMR adoption, it will take a new generation who grew up with connectivity, the Internet, YouTube, and Facebook to embrace such constant, real-time connectivity and all the benefits it will bring. Our children are called "digital natives" because for them the world never existed without these technologies. They will adopt them more quickly than many of us over 40. But there is hope for us, too. I now talk to my kids on the phone less than I text with them. The mother of one of my colleagues would never have dipped her toe into social media. But if she wants to keep up with her grandkids, and know what's happening with her children, Facebook is the best place to find out, so she's become proficient. Yet another friend can't always reach his twenty-something son on his cell phone, but he always gets in touch when he receives a Twitter message from Dad. Our kids are training us in the skills we will need to adopt these new ways of consuming health care and participating in our health. When it happens, we'll all be stronger for it.

Rx for Good Health: No Waiting with mHealth

Mobile health, or mHealth, is a subset of digital health. It is a term broadly used to describe the delivery of health care through mobile devices and multimedia. Increasingly, patients and physicians are adopting smartphones as a mode for research, to track health data, send secure e-mail, exchange images, schedule appointments, and more.

But mHealth can also make gathering tiny, everyday pieces of health information seamlessly simple. Then, it takes care of transmitting and analyzing the pieces so that you and your doctor have an accurate picture of the state of your health on an ongoing basis.

Instead of capturing snapshots of your health at infrequent medical appointments, you and your doctor get a movie. When this happens, every bit of data—your morning blood pressure, that second helping of fudge ripple ice cream you had last night, or the pound you lost last week—becomes meaningful, because it's part of a bigger picture. These bits of data go beyond what you might enter into your iPhone, using other types of clinical monitoring devices today.

The wellness potential is enormous. If you're healthy, digital health technology can help you stay in tip-top shape. If you've got a chronic health condition, digital health monitoring can help you get the upper hand at last. If you're elderly or disabled, digital health and your care team will be able to support your efforts to remain independent and healthy in your own home. And if you just want to lose a few pounds, eat healthier, or improve your mood, there's an app for that, too. Here's what I mean:

- **Easing heart-felt worries**. More than a million Americans have had pacemakers or implanted defibrillators "installed" in their chests to help their hearts maintain a steady rhythm. A big concern: Making adjustments fast if your ticker needs a little more help. Enter "talking" heart-monitoring devices. Widely used in the United States and recently approved in the European Union for people with pacemakers and implanted defibrillators, these wireless units automatically transmit heart-rhythm readings from your chest directly to your doctor's office. Faster care? You bet. A recent Cleveland Clinic–led study of 1,312 people with heart devices has found that remote monitoring alerted doctors to heart rhythm problems in less than 3 days, compared to 30 days for people who were followed at conventional office checks. The bonus: convenience. In the same study, people with remote monitoring systems saw their doctors in the office for scheduled check-ups half as often as those without these systems.[7]

- **A sweeter deal for diabetes**. About one in three of the nation's 24 million people with diabetes is still struggling to keep their blood sugar under control. The "diabetes phone" could help. This cell phone, still a prototype in the United States, has an embedded electronic biosensor that reads glucose levels in a blood sample, then sends the info to your doctor's office. Your doctor can then respond with medication changes or lifestyle advice. One version, marketed in Korea, helped people with type 2 diabetes lower their blood-sugar levels significantly— reducing their risk for diabetes-related complications like nerve damage, kidney failure, and vision loss, report researchers from the Catholic University of Korea. Are we ready for the diabetes phone in the United States? Bring it on! In a study of 202 parents of children with diabetes, published in the November 2009 issue of the *Journal of Diabetes Science and Technology*, 70 percent told

Harvard Medical School researchers they're in favor of diabetes phones to help their doctors better track their children's health.[8]

- **Easier breathing with lung problems**. If you have asthma or another common lung condition called Chronic Obstructive Pulmonary Disease, regular home monitoring of lung health could save your life. Breathing checks can catch problems early, giving your doctor time to change your medication. But it takes more than testing to know what's happening—you and your doctor must be able to interpret the results. At least one wireless medical monitoring device company, the Scottsdale, Arizona–based MedApps, reports work on gadgets that can automatically transmit results from home asthma testing to your electronic medical records and to your doctor. This kind of telemonitoring has a proven return on investment: In one Canadian review, published in 2009 in *The American Journal of Managed Care*, researchers found that asthma patients whose results were sent wirelessly to their doctors were 48 percent less likely to have sleep disturbances or limits on daily activities due to breathing problems.[9]

- **A pill bottle that won't let you miss a dose**. Forgot to take your low-dose aspirin for your heart today? A "smart" pill bottle will remind you—and even tell your spouse. Not taking medication as directed—an issue doctors call "noncompliance"—is a common and serious problem that doubles the risk of death from conditions like heart disease and diabetes. One smart bottle now on the market sends signals to a base station in your home. Forget a scheduled dose and the station blinks. If you don't respond, it chimes. If you still don't get the message, it alerts you—and a designated friend or relative— by phone.

- **Instant-messaging for depression**. You don't have to be a whizzy computer geek to use the online counseling program at England's University of Bristol, researchers say. When 300 people with depression, ages 30 to 70, tried 10 sessions of computer-based instant-messaging therapy with a counselor or traditional, face-to-face therapy, researchers found the online sessions were 2½ times more likely to lead to recovery. Lead researcher David Kessler of the University of Bristol says the program was easy to use and ideal for anyone who's homebound, disabled, or lives far from their therapist.[10]

Convenience? Sure. Better health? Absolutely. And it takes both to deliver the service and quality that we expect as patients. These technologies are here today and are beginning to make a difference for millions of people. It won't be long before every phone has these features built in. All we have to do is turn them on.

Mobile Health Is Personal Health

With EMRs and HIEs (health information exchanges), health IT is playing on a bigger stage, but the concepts and tools behind digital health will bring things back to a personal level. Digital health is built on super-easy technology that already exists: smartphones, tablet computers, web cameras, and high-def television. The next step is taking healthcare mobile. mHealth devices—anything from a talking heart monitor to a diabetes phone—transmit and analyze everyday health data without the individual having to do much of anything.

We have already turned on other familiar technology to connect doctors and patients, even when they are miles apart. Telehealth is one of the most exciting. It goes beyond telemedicine—which is itself already proving its capacity to improve the well-being of large populations—to support long-distance clinical support and the digital exchange of information. I'll explore both of these developments next.

Notes

1. "Healthcare Practices Embrace Mobile Technologies, New CompTIA Research Reveals," CompTIA Press Release, November 24, 2011, www.scoop.it/t/mobile-healthcare/p/717362006/press-releases-healthcare-practices-embrace-mobile-technologies-new-comptia-research-reveals.

2. Lydia Zepeda, "Think before You Eat: Photographic Food Diaries as Intervention Tools to Change Dietary Decision Making and Attitudes," *International Journal of Consumer Studies*, 32 (2008): 692–698, onlinelibrary.wiley.com/doi/10.1111/j.1470-6431.2008.00725.x/abstract.

3. Megan Johnson, "Visiting Your Doctor Online Is a Virtual Reality," *US News & World Report*, October 27, 2009, http://health.usnews.com/health-news/family-health/articles/2009/10/27/visiting-your-doctor-online-is-a-virtual-reality.

4. Emma Schwartz, "Can Cleveland Clinic Be a Model for Digital Medicine?" *Huffington Post Investigative Fund*, www.huffingtonpost.com/2009/12/02/can-cleveland-clinic-be-a_n_376842.html.

5. D. Alan Lankford, "Wireless CPAP Patient Monitoring: Accuracy Study," *Telemedicine Journal and e-Health* 10, no. 2 (Summer 2004): 162–169, doi:10.1089/tmj.2004.10.162, http://online.liebertpub.com/doi/abs/10.1089/tmj.2004.10.162.

6. Roger Orpwood, Bath Institute of Medical Engineering, University of Bath, UK, "Smart Homes," *International Encyclopedia of Rehabilitation*, http://cirrie.buffalo.edu/encyclopedia/en/article/155/.

7. TRUST Trial Confirms Early Detection of Cardiac Events (Using ICDs with Remote Monitoring), www.biotronik.com/files/6D7A911740AB4159C1257886003DAA54/$FILE/Press%20release%20TRUSTwith%20presentation.pdf, and Haran Burri, "Remote

Monitoring and Follow-Up of Pacemakers and Implantable Cardioverter Defibrillators," *Europace* 11, no. 6 (2009): 701–709, www.ncbi.nlm.nih.gov/pmc/articles/PMC2686319/.

8. Venessa Pena, "Mobile Phone Technology for Children with Type 1 and Type 2 Diabetes: A Parent Survey," *Journal of Diabetes Science and Technology* 3, no. 6 (November 2009), www.journalofdst.org/November2009/Articles/VOL-3-6-CLA1-PENA.pdf.

9. Mirou Jaana, "Home Telemonitoring for Respiratory Conditions: A Systematic Review," *The American Journal of Managed Care* 15 (May 2009): 313–320, www.ajmc.com/publications/issue/2009/2009-05-vol15-n5/AJMC_09May_Jaana_313to320/4.

10. David Kessler, "Therapist-Delivered Internet Psychotherapy for Depression in Primary Care: A Randomised Controlled Trial," *The Lancet* 374 (2009): 628–634, www.nationalstressclinic.com/wp-content/uploads/lancet-study.pdf.

Chapter 5

Connected Care Teams

Delivering Care via Technology

It's Wednesday morning, and Dr. Future is swooshing down a ski slope in the Rocky Mountains when her cell phone vibrates in a series of short pulses. This modern Morse code provides her cue that a patient requires attention. She pauses on the ski lift to glance at the device. A real-time monitoring app on the smartphone shows that Patient Smith's blood pressure has spiked for the second time today. Dr. Future taps Patient Smith's name on the screen to access his medical record. He's an elderly male, living alone. The prescription for his blood pressure medication was set to renew a few days ago, but another tap on the screen shows that the new prescription has not been filled. With one swipe of her finger,

Dr. Future requests a home health nurse to check in on the patient and deliver the prescription.

Next, Dr. Future takes a moment to answer a text message from another patient, who wonders if he should be concerned about a sudden rash whose onset coincided with his first dose of a new drug. Dr. Future zooms in on the photo the patient has sent. It's a classic allergic rash, so Dr. Future sends an instant message that, in a single step, informs the patient of the diagnosis and requests Dr. Future's triage manager to arrange for the necessary care. A few minutes later, Dr. Future is back on the slopes and two patients are receiving potentially life-saving care.

In the age of real-time health care, technology will not only facilitate more immediate care, it will allow healthcare providers to be less tethered to their offices, better informed about their patients and their histories, more able to consult more efficiently with colleagues, and capable of engaging with patients from anywhere. Seen from home, via video, voice mail, e-mail, and photographs, every type of media can become part of the engagement model. Information from inside and outside the organization can converge in a way that it's an asset to the physician in the moment. Care providers will no longer be confined, 24/7, to the hospital or clinic, but they'll need to adopt new ways to manage their time when they have the potential to be communicating with patients on a continuous basis.

Traditionally, doctors interacted with patients in a single way—the patient came to the office and the two met face-to-face. Whether a patient needed his medication adjusted, a vital sign checked, or simple reassurance that the course of his disease is normal, the old system required the patient to phone ahead to make an appointment, then wait for his appointed day to arrive. But that's an inefficient way to deliver care, especially when the patient's need isn't a physical exam, but a prescription or an expedient medical decision. Given access to something as simple as a secure messaging platform and a robust EMR, healthcare providers can deliver this care immediately with fewer hassles. This is happening today at Kaiser Permanente to the tune of more than 12 million secure messages a year from patients to doctors and back again to resolve simple medical needs without the hours of time or expense of gasoline associated with an office visit.

Telehealth for One-Stop Care

Telehealth—the use of technology supporting long-distance clinical health care and electronic information exchange—will vastly improve how care is delivered. (Not to be confused with telemedicine, a more narrow definition that refers to the delivery of care through telecommunications.) Telehealth's immense potential to improve care has already been demonstrated by Kaiser Permanente and the Veterans Health Administration (VHA), which both use a telehealth model to support patient care. At Kaiser Permanente, telehealth lets members experience true one-stop care. They can see their primary care physician, consult with a specialist, and receive their prescribed medication from the on-site pharmacy, all on the same day. The full potential and convenience of telehealth is uniquely suited to Kaiser Permanente's integrated care model, but the implications are far-reaching. This patient-centered approach, bolstered by the supporting technology, reduces the risk of delays to patient diagnosis and treatment. Pilot projects started in dermatology and orthopedics, where specialists were in great demand and often not located convenient to patients. But now we deploy telehealth for cardiology, allergy, oncology, cosmetic surgery, nephrology, and other specialty practices.

The VHA program centers on a care coordinator, who supports and constantly monitors a panel of 100 to 150 patients. The coordinator's goal is to monitor patient progress, empower patients, and facilitate self-management. Using remote monitoring systems for collecting vital signs, symptom tracking, and medication or therapy adherence monitoring, a single care coordinator can provide services to a much larger number of patients than was ever possible using traditional, face-to-face interactions. The VHA system also brings the patient into the care loop, and provides nudges and support to encourage patients to take a greater role in managing their own health.

The Kaiser Permanente and VHA models work; research shows they improve patient satisfaction and reduce hospital admissions and hospital bed days. At Kaiser Permanente, telehealth results in fewer office visits and significantly shorter wait times for members—many of whom might choose to postpone consultation and treatment rather than deal with challenging travel circumstances. Of the patients who needed to consult with a specialist, 67 percent could consult with the specialist on the same day as their initial primary care physician visit. And about a third of the office-visit referrals for dermatology were eliminated.

The electronic health records adopted by the VHA facilitate optimal telehealth efficiency. Approximately 43,000 veteran patients received care from the VHA's Care Coordination/Home Telehealth (CCHT) program in 2010. These programs, provided via 140 VA Medical Centers, allow the VHA to provide expedient care to patients who live far away from a VA Medical Center. About 40 percent of the patients who received care through the program in 2010 were living in rural or remote locations.

Other practices and organizations around the country are adopting technologies that allow them to make virtual house visits. The Georgia Partnership for TeleHealth is one group promoting such technology. Its Smart House Calls program,[1] based in Watkinsville, Georgia, provides a system for physicians to connect with their patients online in real time, without an actual office visit. Using video and audio technology, a physician delivers the care needed, and the patient avoids spending any more time than necessary in a potentially infectious waiting room. Software allows doctors to share information, including test results and diagnostic images, with their patients in a confidential, secure manner. The Smart House Calls technology provides a model for the future—it requires no downloads, no expensive hardware, and it's easy and intuitive to use.

Telehealth is already reducing costly emergency room visits in one Georgia community. Paula Guy, CEO of the Georgia Partnership for TeleHealth, told the *Atlanta Journal-Constitution* that a new telehealth program implemented in Berrien County in south Georgia reduced the number of asthma-related emergency room visits among children from 44 in 2010 to just one in 2011.[2]

Telehealth also promises to provide cost-effective ways to access specialized services. In 2005, for instance, the VHA instituted a program of teleretinal imaging, which allows digital retinal imaging (to screen for diabetic retinopathy, a preventable complication from diabetes that provides a biomarker for other types of organ deterioration related to the disease). Doctors involved in the Georgia Partnership for TeleHealth are using devices like high-definition cameras, Bluetooth stethoscopes, and mobile apps to diagnose conditions such as ear infections and heart murmurs. This approach can trim costs by cutting back on unnecessary visits.

There aren't too many situations in life where everyone is a winner. These technologies are speeding us to a time when people are healthy and happier, physicians and staff are more effective and productive, and the entire health system is more affordable. All with fewer errors and higher quality than we ever thought was possible.

In the Hospital

One place where telehealth has already begun to make a major difference is in the intensive care unit (ICU). Statistics show that the ICU represents health care's highest mortality and greatest costs, and ICU care accounts for about $107 billion in healthcare spending each year.[3] Two troubling trends threaten to make ICUs even more problematic—an aging population that will create more and more potential critical care patients and a falling supply of critical care physicians.

Tele-ICUs, which utilize telemedicine technologies in the ICU, have the potential to drastically increase the productivity of ICU care providers and allow them to service a larger number of patients. The Tele-ICU solves staffing shortages by establishing critical care command centers where trained physicians and specialists can remotely monitor and consult with ICU patients in multiple, geographically dispersed locations. Using remote monitoring systems, people in the command center keep tabs on ICU patients in real time, coordinating care with specialists on-site.

A recent demonstration project in Massachusetts[4] showed that ICU mortality rates dropped as much as 36 percent in hospitals that adopted the Tele-ICU technology. Patient stays in the ICU also fell, by up to 30 percent. Although the Tele-ICU in the Massachusetts study has one-time start-up costs of approximately $7.1 million for a major medical center and $400,000 for community hospitals, these initial costs were paid back in savings within a single year. The Tele-ICUs also saved payers money: about $2,600 per patient.

Telemedicine: A Changing Role

Until recently, telemedicine—the delivery of care through telecommunications—was merely an effective way to deliver specialized services, like dermatology, one-on-one to remote, underserved areas. But at Kaiser Permanente, telemedicine has expanded into exciting new applications that can affect the well-being of large populations. It spans a broad continuum of care from teleconsultation to chronic condition management. Patients can teleconsult with a specialist in real time, with their primary care physician sitting in on the consultation. This patient-centered approach, bolstered by the supporting technology, reduces the risk of delays to patient diagnosis and treatment

In Northern California, the Virtual Roving Dermatologist program was developed to increase the number of teleconsultations offered to a patient on the same day as she met with her primary care physician. A pilot in one Northern California service area showed that 67 percent of the patients who needed to could teleconsult with a specialist on the same day they saw their primary care physician. Of patients who consulted with the Virtual Roving Dermatologist, 71 percent would use the service again.

Telemedicine has been piloted for orthopedic and spine consultations, as well as in clinical decision support. For example, Kaiser Permanente medical facilities in Virginia can now connect with an orthopedic specialist at any time via video. Without this capability, some Kaiser Permanente members in the Mid-Atlantic region would have had to travel 62 miles to see an orthopedist. Teleconsultations also mean seeing a specialist sooner than you would in person, often on the day the referral is made.

Telemedicine also lets members experience true one-stop care. They can see their primary care physician, consult with a specialist, and order their prescribed medication for overnight delivery, all on the same day and from the comfort of their own homes. The prescriptions can even be delivered by mail. With all the advantages that telemedicine offers, it is not surprising that it is being used for an increasing variety of applications.

In rural areas of Pennsylvania, an interactive voice response (IVR) system and other telemonitoring tools are keeping recently discharged patients out of the hospital. And, according to a recent study of over 3,200 members of the Geisinger Health Plan, those whose health was monitored this way were 44 percent less likely to wind up back in the hospital within a month.

Patients used the keypad on their telephones to answer yes or no to questions that would reveal post-discharge problems, including queries about eating and drinking habits, breathing, wound healing, and whether or not they were taking their medications. What happened next: If a patient noted a problem, such as trouble breathing, a nurse would immediately call and arrange for a doctor's appointment if needed.

The program is used by a wide variety of patients with diseases including diabetes, cancer, and pneumonia as well as trauma recovery. In addition, heart-failure patients are also monitored remotely via weight and blood-pressure measuring devices that send data back to Geisinger via Bluetooth technology. A sudden rise in weight can indicate worsening of the condition. So if a patient's weight changes by more than a preset number of pounds, an alert is sounded. Patients may be told to take more of their diuretic medication or be asked to see their doctor, pronto.[5,6]

Changing Practices

How will these new technologies be integrated into daily practice? Clinicians will make decisions about which technologies to adopt based on usability, convenience, interactive integration, security, cost, and support, and they'll use these factors to determine each technology's value to the organization and to patients. Ideally, technology should be so easy that there's no training or manuals, and it takes minutes instead of hours to master—no learning involved. There should be no reason to go into a classroom to learn new technologies that are being introduced to support health care, and the minimal need for training will save time and money over the costly way we implement new technologies today.

Increasingly, healthcare business decisions will be made by business leaders in partnership with clinicians, who together understand all the pieces that need to come together, including the clinical and technical sides of the business. More physicians are going into leadership roles, and the health systems with the best outcomes are those with strong clinician leadership. Doctors and technology leaders are already collaborating, and have been for many years, to determine the right set of capabilities for the future. One major theme that will continue to emerge with even greater emphasis is the need to connect care. Connecting care should allow us to eliminate over half a trillion dollars in duplicate services and tests being done today. If we must connect care, then emerging medical devices must adopt a fundamental characteristic—they must have the ability to connect.

As new technologies emerge, we'll see medical practices evolving to take advantage of real-time health care. Technology-enabled medical practices will emphasize shift work, and healthcare providers will choose where they work. Clinicians will enjoy the ability to work from anywhere, consulting patients in the morning and fishing in the afternoon. Technology will provide exciting new possibilities for work–life balance.

Fewer and fewer physicians today are solo practitioners, and soon enough, small, stand-alone islands of medical practice will be a thing of the past. In their place, we will see more integrated care delivered by teams coalescing around their areas of service and medical specialties. These teams may look like your familiar local doctor's practice, but they will have more purchasing power to obtain the technology to drive better health outcomes and efficiency.

We are already seeing this with the adoption of relatively inexpensive electronic medical record systems. In addition, innovation will reduce the cost to physicians over time as the technology sector finds ways to deliver technical capabilities at an affordable price point. Expanding the use of technology in health care represents tremendous financial opportunity for technologists and business leaders. But it would be a mistake to interpret that as another burden on the backs of the health care consuming public. If it is done right—by technology leaders, physicians, healthcare systems, the government, and consumers—the care coordination, secure sharing of information, and the ability to capitalize on mobile modes of the doctor-patient relationship that is enabled by the technology will ultimately save the system—and consumers—money.

Having information available at the right time and in the right place drives better health outcomes. Better health reduces costly emergency room care and the myriad of care costs associated with chronic conditions that can be avoided.

But there are some things we must do to ensure this virtuous cycle meets its full potential. First, we have to get the cost of the technology out of the operations. We must invest in single, standardized, and standards-based systems that can be upgraded at a pace in keeping with the pace of technology and that are capable of connecting more easily to other systems. There is a gold mine of efficiency to be realized there. And we cannot continue to build asset-intensive hospitals and medical office buildings and hope that the very people who cannot afford care will fill them. We must think differently about how care is delivered in this new age of technology and adjust our operations to meet the patients where they are. (See Figure 5.1.)

I believe medical practices will change in several important ways.

- Technology will enable doctors and nurses to care for more patients over wider areas. Geography will become less and less of a limiting factor for good medical care. Still, the federal government has archaic standards for geo-access that tend to reinforce the old model. Regulatory reform will be essential to allowing these critical changes to take flight and bring the improved outcomes

- Hospitals and medical groups will restructure their human resources and employ new staff. Large healthcare plans are already recruiting people for positions with titles like "health data analyst" who engage directly with these new technologies. These analysts will provide more technical expertise at a lower cost than a physician.

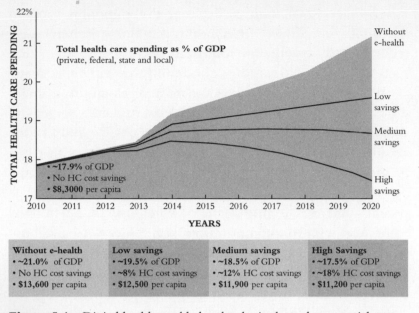

Figure 5.1 Digital health–enabled technologies have the potential to flatten the cost curve.
SOURCE: Centers for Medicare and Medicaid Services; U.S. Census Bureau; Bain & Company analysis.

Some doctors may be hired specifically to monitor and work with virtual diagnostics, whereas others might focus most of their time delivering video-based visits to patients. Additionally, these analysts will be the people using the vast troves of data to find that next breakthrough, whether that be in treatment, efficiency, work flow, or safety. Their ability to understand the practice of medicine as well as their capabilities with math and technology will enable them to look for patterns others won't see. These patterns in the data will lead to more and better understanding of disease and give us new knowledge about how to treat it.

• Technology will be simple to learn and potentially have self-healing capabilities. Scenarios where a robot breaks and then fixes itself will become commonplace. That sounds like science fiction, but complex computer systems are beginning to carry these self-healing capabilities now. Like every consumer with a laptop at home, those in the healthcare profession want technology that doesn't require lengthy and complicated calls to tech support.

- Home care will increasingly be supported remotely by robots that can respond to voice commands and monitor patient status. Some robots in current development may even prevent falls in elderly patients.
- The cost of implementing new technology will fall, because everything just works and it's easy to pick up and use. Simplicity will rule design and usability will soar in response. Medical practices will spend less time and money on training.
- Office visits will become a choice among many options. They won't be necessary in all cases, and for those who still prefer face-to-face interaction with their doctor, the office visit will become more meaningful—an extension of the ongoing relationship between doctor and patient made possible by technology. They'll be less rushed, more informative, and drive better health outcomes. All of this will make medical practice more rewarding.

This sounds like a description of a faraway place, somewhere in the distant future. But these technologies are here today. They're not well integrated. They are far from elegant. They lack the human-centered design that will ultimately prove their worth. But companies are creating mobile apps for health care today. In many cases, they pay small amounts of money to have the work of others assembled into new products or applications, and then sell those as innovations. This is why the app generation has been so quick to create capabilities.

One app is built on the success of another. Before we know it, the future has been created, and we are all benefiting.

Where Do We Go from Here?

Some challenges still remain. The current economic model is a barrier—fee for service does not provide incentives for the adoption of technology. But remote technologies will become standard, nonetheless. A recent BBC Research report predicts that the global telemedicine market will grow from $9.8 billion in 2010 to "to $27.3 billion in 2016, a compound annual growth rate (CAGR) of 18.6 percent over the next five years."[7]

Physicians will need to overcome their own biases, especially the view that health care has to be face-to-face to be deeply personal, when the technologies are allowing them to reach more patients interactively in a shorter period via something as simple as e-mail. As the technology to connect becomes more widely used and acceptable, face-to-face visits will take on a whole new meaning. The new normal will include virtual, video-based, as well as physical visits. Ultimately, doctors will find that their productivity is enhanced, and they gain the ability to heal more people and touch more people's lives in a personal way, but these changes may alter their vision of how health care is delivered. For those of us in health care, our vision must shift to align with the lens of the patient. Patients at Kaiser Permanente tell us that using mobile capabilities to manage their health and interact with their care team makes health care more personal, not less. They are more connected to their doctor than ever before. Our entire system is in the palm of their hands with our mobile apps. Patients are adjusting quickly. We have to do the same. My colleagues at Kaiser Permanente have had more than 10 years of secure online interactions with patients. They feel the same way patients do. These interactions have made them champions of caring for patients wherever they are.

The path ahead is clear, though change is difficult for individuals and institutions alike. A physician for whom I have enormous respect reminds me on occasion that doctors are taught that to be a good doctor, you must see, hear, and touch your patients. That's true in many cases. There are many more cases where virtual capabilities can support the delivery of expert care at greater convenience and decreased cost to the patient.

We've created a world for ourselves through mobile and social media where connecting is virtual. Whatever we think of it, physical interactions are limited in comparison to our ability to reach out, and often truly connect as humans, through networks and technology. A young doctor recently said to me, "Why should I personally see a small number of patients when I went to medical school to help as many people as I can? These technologies bridge time and space. They enable me to see more patients in a single day than would have otherwise been possible. I can use telemedicine and skip the freeway traffic between our medical facilities. I went to medical school to help people. Not to sit in traffic."

Helping as Many People as We Can

Telehealth—the use of technology supporting long-distance clinical health care and electronic information exchange—and telemedicine—the delivery of care through telecommunications—are already improving care in many settings. In Georgia, doctors use high-def cameras, Bluetooth stethoscopes, and mobile apps to diagnose ear infections and heart murmurs in a remote visit instead of an office visit. Using Tele-ICU technology reduced intensive-care-unit mortality rates by as much as 36 percent in a Massachusetts demonstration project.

Telemedicine also pays dividends. Research at the Veterans Health Administration and Kaiser Permanente shows that telemedicine improves patient satisfaction, reduces hospital admissions and hospital bed days, and results in fewer office visits and shorter wait times before getting an appointment.

These technologies will require a culture change, especially for physicians who believe that health care has to be face-to-face to be deeply personal. It also will mean shifting to a model where decisions are made by business leaders in partnership with clinicians, decisions that marry the clinical and technical sides of health care. More physicians are going into leadership roles, and the health systems with the best outcomes are those with strong clinician leadership.

Done thoughtfully and methodically, the transformation of health care can help my colleague achieve his goal of helping as many people as he can. I want to help him do just that in the way I know best: with technology. So do the other players in the transformation of healthcare IT: the health plans and insurers who help pay for health care, the government that regulates and mandates care, and most importantly, the private sector, whose proven ability to fill unmet needs with innovation will deliver.

Notes

1. "Smart House Calls Program," http://smarthousecalls.com/.
2. Georgia Partnership for TeleHealth, "Telemedicine Becoming the New House Call," April 17, 2012. www.gatelehealth.org/index.php/2012/04/telemedicine-becoming-the-new-house-call/

3. "Critical Care, Critical Choices: The Case for Tele-ICUs in Intensive Care," New England Healthcare Institute and Massachusetts Technology Collaborative, December 2010, www.masstech.org/agencyoverview/mtc_reports/teleICU.pdf.

4. Ibid.

5. J. Graham, "Postdischarge Monitoring Using Interactive Voice Response System Reduces 30-Day Readmission Rates in a Case-Managed Medicare Population," *Medical Care* 50, no. 1 (January 2012): 50–57, www.ncbi.nlm.nih.gov/pubmed/21822152.

6. AMC Health Press Release, "Geisinger Health Plan and AMC Health Find Success with Remote Patient Monitoring," February 2012, https://amchealth.com/uploads/PressRelease__GHP_and_AMC_Health_Find_Success_with_Remote_Patient_Monitoring_FINAL___v02282012.pdf.

7. "Global Markets for Telemedicine Technologies," BBC Research report, March, 2012, www.bccresearch.com/report/telemedicine-technologies-global-markets-hlc014e.html.

Chapter 6

Three Key Players Driving Healthcare IT Innovation

Good-bye, game shows: Watson, the famous IBM supercomputer that trounced the competition on the TV show *Jeopardy!* has a day job. Watson drew big TV audiences and taught America an important lesson about information technology's ability to gather and analyze enormous amounts of data. Now, Watson's teaming up with health benefits company WellPoint to become a physician's assistant.

In collaboration with cancer specialists at the Cedars Sinai Cancer Institute in Los Angeles, Watson will use its supercomputing prowess (it can take in 200 million pages of content in just three seconds[1]) to review cancer research and outcomes. The goal: Mine huge amounts of oncology data so doctors know more about best practices and can better manage patient care.[2] If successful, and this is a big if, the potential impact on the health of cancer patients and over-all improvements to our knowledge in the field of oncology could be miraculous. It has the potential to advance medical science decades in just years. This is where we all hope information tools and advanced supercomputers will take us.

When one of America's biggest names in computing joins forces with America's largest publicly traded health insurer (WellPoint runs Blue Cross Blue Shield plans in 14 states), you know we're headed for powerful new health IT possibilities. "It's like having 1,000 consulting physicians backing up the clinician, whether the clinician is located in an academic center in a regional medical center or a community hospital," said Harlan Levine, executive vice president for comprehensive health solutions at WellPoint, when Watson's new job was announced in 2011.[3] "This very much fits into the sweet spot of what we envisioned for the applications of Watson," Manoj Saxena, an IBM general manager, told the Associated Press.[4]

Watson in a white jacket. It's a great illustration of how some of the key players driving healthcare IT innovation are getting down to business. Watson beat his *Jeopardy!* competitors to the buzzer, but it will take the combined power of payers, private industry, and government to bring home big health IT victories. The good news is we're already winning at this game. Here's how these three big players are contributing.

Government: Rewarding Success Instead of Funding Failure

"Meaningful use" was a term scarcely used in health care before 2009; Google it today and you'll get at least 2 million hits. Your doctor and administrators at your local hospital now think about meaningful use all the time. What does it mean? Quite simply, it is translating healthcare standards into practice—a great definition provided by the University of Vermont's Center for Clinical and Translational Science in a June 2012 paper in the *Journal of Biomedical Informatics*.[5] In terms of the discussion in this book, meaningful use demands that care providers go beyond merely implementing an electronic health record, and put it to good use caring for patients to qualify for government funding.

The current system rewards any service or output—good or bad—which is a perverse and ineffective way to run any system, much less one in which failure can cost lives and increase human suffering. If we cause sepsis in a hospital, the hospital gets paid many times more to cure it, if it can. At Kaiser Permanente, we saw sepsis as preventable and focused our care teams on reducing it. We don't make money when patients are sick. We make money by keeping them well. Our care teams used our electronic health records to evaluate various approaches and implement the best options across our hospitals. The result of this evidence-based approach: We reduced sepsis mortality by more than 40 percent.

Ultimately, meaningful use will translate into better health for you, your family, your community, and our nation. But it won't happen overnight. Meaningful use will happen in stages (shown in Figure 6.1):

Stage 1: Data capture and sharing. Electronic capture of health information in a structured format; Stage 1 began in 2011.

Stage 2: Advanced clinical processes. Quality improvement at the point of care and electronic exchange of information; Stage 2 is scheduled to begin in 2013.

STAGE 1	STAGE 2	STAGE 3
2011–2012	2013	2015
Data capture and sharing	Advance clinical processes	Improved outcomes
Meaningful use criteria focus on:		
Electronically capturing health information in a standardized format	More rigorous health information exchange (HIE)	Improving quality, safety, and efficiency, leading to improved health outcomes
Using that information to track key clinical conditions	Increased requirements for e-prescribing and incorporating lab results	Decision support for national high-priority conditions
Communicating that information for care coordination processes	Electronic transmission of patient care summaries across multiple settings	Patient access to self-management tools
Initiating the reporting of clinical quality measures and public health information	More patient-controlled data	Access to comprehensive patient data through patient-centered HIE
Using information to engage patients and their families in their care		Improving population health

Figure 6.1 Each stage in the implementation of meaningful use will move us from putting systems in place to connecting the systems to seeing their effect on our nation's health.

SOURCE: ONC http://www.healthit.gov/providers-professionals/how-attain-meaningful-use.

Stage 3: Improved outcomes. Improvements in quality, safety, and efficiency; clinical decision support and patient self-management tools; Stage 3 is slated to begin in 2015.

What this means for our nation's health becomes more clear when you look at some of the detailed meaningful use criteria issued by the Centers for Medicare and Medicaid (CMS), which is part of the Department of Health and

Human Services. Within the realm of healthcare IT, that list includes logging drug orders electronically (computerized provider order entry); using e-prescribing to generate and transmit permissible prescriptions electronically; exchanging key clinical information electronically with other doctors, specialists, and institutions; and providing timely electronic access to a patient's health information, among other criteria.

Yes, it's a big job for busy physicians and hospitals. Via carrots and sticks for Medicare and Medicaid health delivery, meaningful use will contribute to the transformation of health care for the rest of us, too. It creates a growing market, plus a huge need for hundreds if not thousands of innovative solutions large and small that can be filled by creative minds in private industry. It's a perfect storm for growth that will address a basic human need.

Government can and does step in to stop our system's habit of rewarding failure. Without this push, the healthcare system would never change on its own.

Government: Guardrails, Handrails, and Connectors

Government also can provide guardrails to protect us and handrails to encourage innovation. By this, I mean providing mandates and incentives for success. While I believe that the private sector ultimately must correct our healthcare system, government does have a role to protect us from a system that, left to itself, would do more harm than good, possibly bankrupting the country with little room for improvement. Thus, the health insurance mandate included in the Affordable Care Act is an important mandate, or guardrail, in that it gives as many Americans as possible access to health insurance and the care they need.

Setting standards for great care that rewards success (measured in terms of better health, not just in healthcare dollars saved) rather than continuing to reward failure is another appropriate guardrail the government can put in place.

Government incentives that encourage nationwide adoption of EHR systems and the widespread connection of these systems are much-needed handrails that will allow healthcare organizations of all sizes and shapes to participate fully in the evolution of healthcare technology.

Efforts to link systems are now under way—often using the secure, standards-based protocols spearheaded by another noteworthy, government-spearheaded effort: the DIRECT project, started in 2010.[6] DIRECT showcases the government's role as a connector. This public–private collaboration was jump-started by the Health and Human Services Office of the National Coordinator for Health Information Technology. Its goal is to identify a simple, secure, scalable, standards-based way for participants to send authenticated, encrypted health information directly to known, trusted recipients over the Internet.

Dozens of companies—all competitors in this growing field—and health organizations joined forces for this unique, open-source collaboration. Participating companies included Allscripts, Cerner, Epic, General Electric, Google, IBM, Intel, Microsoft, NextGen, Siemens, and Surescripts.[7]

The standards they set rely on Internet-based e-mail and public key encryption technology. To enhance security, no personally identifiable information is used in headers, and attachments can be opened only by the message recipient. This secure, direct clinical messaging allows healthcare providers to stop using printers, fax machines, the postal service, and unsecure e-mail to move patient information. And it's making a difference across the country in projects including these three:

1. The VisionShare project has allowed the Hennepin County (Minnesota) Medical Center to send vaccination data easily and securely to the Minnesota Department of Health.[8]

2. The Rhode Island Quality Institute (RIQI) is using the new standards to spur data exchange between primary care doctors and specialists, and to link physicians' medical records with CurrentCare, the state's health information exchange (HIE).[9]

3. HealthBridge, a Cincinnati-based health IT provider that works with nine medical centers in the Greater Cincinnati area and others in Indiana, is helping local and even some far-flung health organizations communicate via secure direct e-mail. In early 2012, the new standards allowed a Bloomington, Indiana hospital to e-mail a family physician with information about a newly discharged patient. The demonstration involved a virtual patient, named Joanna Hoosierfan, whose local healthcare provider works with Margaret Mary Community Hospital in Batesville, Indiana and uses HealthBridge for HIE. Joanna was in Bloomington, Indiana for a sporting event and ended up in the ER at Indiana University Health Bloomington Hospital with shortness of breath. "The reality is patients travel and get care from different healthcare providers in different places," noted Keith Hepp, interim CEO for HealthBridge. "That means that our healthcare IT systems need to be able to share information more easily with each other and with the patient."[10]

The DIRECT Project[11] is a great example of what I believe is the best way for government to influence the future of great healthcare IT, by giving the private sector the support to find and test solutions on its own.

Government: Seed Money for Healthcare IT

Government can direct public funds to jump-start innovation, but it should not dictate the solutions that private industry will develop or that providers and payers will ultimately choose and use. Indeed, this should be seen as seed money, with healthcare consumers and the private sector reaping the benefits and the profits down the line.

HITECH Help

February 17, 2009 will be remembered as a major turning point for healthcare IT in America. That day, President Obama signed into law the $789-billion economic stimulus package called the American Recovery and Reinvestment Act (ARRA). Doctors, hospitals, health insurers, patients, and the health IT community took notice because ARRA included the Health Information Technology for Economic and Clinical Health Act (HITECH): $19 billion in incentives (both carrots and sticks) for doctors and hospitals that adopt electronic health records, then use them in meaningful ways.

The goals? First, an EHR for each person in the United States by 2014. Second, the development of a nationwide health information technology infrastructure that allows for the electronic use and exchange of information. But not just any digital medical file or any level of interconnection will do. The government is insisting—via incentives and, later, penalties—that physicians and hospitals demonstrate that their new systems have the capability to improve patient health, at least among Medicare and Medicaid patients.

HITECH pays doctors and hospitals when they adopt EHRs and demonstrate their use in ways that can improve the quality, safety, and effectiveness of care. Eligible professionals can receive as much as $44,000 over a five-year period through Medicare. For Medicaid, eligible professionals can receive as much as $63,750 over six years. HITECH incentives are paid on a per-provider basis. For example, a practice with two physicians and a nurse practitioner using an EHR could qualify for $132,000 in Medicare incentives. Incentive payments for eligible hospitals began in 2011 with base payments of $2 million.

The stick? Beginning in 2015, physicians who elect not to use an EHR will be penalized, starting with a 1 percent Medicare fee reduction. The fee reduction rises to 3 percent after 2017 for those who do not adopt an EHR. Hospitals face penalties as well. The impact will be felt beyond our 50 states and the District of Columbia. HITECH also covers Puerto Rico, the Virgin Islands, Guam, American Samoa, and the Northern Mariana Islands.

The road's been bumpy at times, but HITECH is working. The number of physicians and hospitals with EHRs has skyrocketed in just a few short years. At press time, the latest numbers from the Centers for Disease Control and Prevention show that 57 percent of office-based physicians were using at least a basic electronic health record system, with use by state ranging from 40 percent in Louisiana to 84 percent in North Dakota.[12] About 34 percent had systems that met basic government criteria for meaningful use, up from 10.5 percent in 2006. And according to the Office of the Coordinator for Health Information Technology's latest data as of February 2012, 34.8 percent of nonfederal, acute-care hospitals had adopted at least a basic electronic health records system as well—up from just 13.4 percent in 2008.[13]

As the country adopts electronic medical records and they are put to meaningful use, we will be better positioned to deliver better, safer, higher-quality health care to the country. A connected system of EHRs sets up a future where any physician who treats you can have your health history at her fingertips. With this information, care teams will be better able than at any other time in history to arrive at more precise diagnoses and develop faster, more accurate treatment plans for regaining your good health.

Health Care Innovation Awards

Uncle Sam isn't just handing out money so that your doctor or local hospital can buy a fancy computer system. Healthcare providers have to prove they're using their new systems to improve people's health in quantifiable ways.

For healthcare IT to succeed, it must solve real problems and save real money. Private industry's best at this, but government incentives can help level the playing field and let providers test-drive a variety of high-tech solutions. The federal Health Care Innovation Awards program is doing just that. According to Health and Human Services Secretary Kathleen Sebelius, the awards support innovative projects nationwide designed to deliver high-quality medical care, enhance the healthcare workforce, and save money. So far, HHS has made awards to 107 projects with the potential to save the healthcare system $1.9 billion in the next few years.[14]

These awards bring providers and technology together in exciting and practical new ways. Three promising examples are:

1. Sanford One Care: With a $12.1 million award, the Sanford Health system will train providers (including registered-nurse health coaches and behavioral-health therapists) in Iowa, Minnesota, North Dakota, and

South Dakota to provide telehealth services to people at remote clinics. Behavioral health is the missing link that keeps people on track with healthy habits despite all the challenges that everyday life throws at us. Filling this gap could save the Sanford system $14 million.[15]

2. The Institute for Clinical Systems Improvement (ICSI) of Bloomington, Minnesota: The ICSI received a $17.9 million award to improve care delivery and outcomes for high-risk adult patients with Medicare or Medicaid coverage who have depression plus diabetes or cardiovascular disease in California, Colorado, Iowa, Massachusetts, Michigan, Minnesota, Pennsylvania, Washington, and Wisconsin. Savings could approach $27.6 million as patients get help controlling their blood sugar and heart disease despite the pull of depression, which can throw off efforts to take medication, eat healthy, exercise, and see the doctor as recommended.[16]

3. The CHRISTUS St. Michael Health System: A $1.6 million grant to this health system in Texas and Arkansas will fund the Integrated Nurse Training and Mobile Device Harm Reduction Program. It will train nurses to recognize early warning signs of congestive heart failure and sepsis in Medicare beneficiaries in nursing home facilities and elsewhere. It is expected to reduce hospital readmissions due to these conditions by 20 percent and save lives.[17]

Payers: Healthcare Plans and Insurers Enter the EHR Market

In the past few years, media coverage of doctors and hospitals adopting EHR systems has proliferated. But lately, the headlines are telling a new story. Healthcare insurers are investing heavily in healthcare IT, too. By providing connected EHR systems to doctors and hospitals in their networks—systems linked with their own claims records—payers are changing the game. Many insurers are doing this by purchasing EHR systems and offering them to physicians and hospitals, then collaborating with them on care upgrades and cost savings. Some recent examples:

- **Helping providers go digital**. Humana recently announced it will provide financial assistance to selected physicians for the purchase of NextGen® Ambulatory EHR and reward them for improved clinical performance in a program that's part of the health insurer's Medical Home EHR Rewards Program.[18]
- **Powerful IT partnerships**. In February 2012, three of America's leading Blue Cross Blue Shield health plans announced a partnership with health IT provider Lumeris Corp. to acquire NaviNet, the nation's largest real-time communication network for physicians, hospitals, and health insurers. Together, the three "Blues" in on the deal—Highmark, Horizon Blue Cross Blue Shield of New Jersey (Horizon), and Independence Blue Cross (IBC)—work with more than 70,000 physicians and hospitals to deliver care to more than 11 million people. Linking their records in real time via NaviNet will open up new tools for improving the health of millions of Americans.[19]
- **Better EHRs for kids**. In November 2011, United Healthcare of Arizona donated $125,000 to three children's medical facilities for electronic medical records systems, e-prescribing, and practice management capabilities. The three are Tucson Children's Clinics, Flagstaff Medical Center Children's Health Center, and Yuma

Regional Medical Center Children's Rehabilitative Services. "This donation from United Healthcare will help our organization invest in technology and process improvements that will enhance patient care and safety," the Yuma Regional Medical Center President and CEO said at the time. "We appreciate this support and are excited about what this means for residents in Yuma and local children."[20]

- **EHR expansion for North Carolina doctors**. Blue Cross Blue Shield of North Carolina and Chicago-based Allscripts, which creates and markets electronic health records, announced a partnership in 2011 to offer software, training, and support to more than 750 North Carolina physicians, including doctors at 39 free clinics. The $23 million project will help families receive "vital, faster, better care because vital records are available when doctors need them most, wherever a patient might be," Blue Cross President and Chief Executive Brad Wilson said.[21]

Payers see that this kind of investment in electronic records and interconnected systems pushes health care toward a better future. Better systems eliminate duplications and errors, and improve provider communication and patient compliance for a direct impact on the payer's own bottom line. It's a win–win, because great systems improve patient health while saving money.

That's not just a nice theory—it really works. For a great case in point look no further than Michigan, where a collaboration between Blue Cross Blue Shield and 70 hospitals improved care, reduced complications, and saved a reported $232 million. This collaboration is also proof that connected health records between doctors and hospitals build trust and cooperation—important for future collaboration.[22]

Payers Leap into Accountable Care

The concept of an accountable care organization is not new to the people who work for and get care from Kaiser Permanente and a few other organizations such as Geisinger Health Systems. They are a care provider and health plan in one, connected through information technology, paying attention to end-to-end, patient-centered care.

Could accountable care organizations, also called ACOs, be the next big thing in health care? The federal government, doctors, hospitals, and payers are all experimenting with ACOs. The idea is that in a local ACO, primary-care doctors, specialists, and hospitals work together as a team to care for a group of patients. Providers will be held accountable for the cost and quality of that care. The goal is coordinated, efficient care, with funds going to prevention and disease management instead of crisis care in the emergency room and doctor's office.

This kind of proactive care requires a serious investment in good healthcare IT. Who will develop ACOs? Right now, everyone is. The government is developing model programs. Private ACOs are also on the rise—up a whopping 104 percent between November 2011 and August 2012, according to intelligence business firm Leavitt Partners. Of 327 ACOs in existence in August 2012, most (58 percent) were run by hospital systems or physician groups (40 percent). (See Figure 6.2.)[23]

ACOs work by budgeting money for care; providers decide how best to use it. Rather than pay doctors or hospitals each time they provide a service, payers agree—up front—to provide a set amount of money. Providers work together to make the best decisions. Outcomes are monitored and rewarded. Great ACOs require great data-sharing

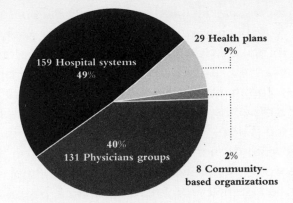

159 Hospital systems
49%

29 Health plans
9%

40%
131 Physicians groups

2%
8 Community-
based organizations

Figure 6.2 To date, hospitals lead the way in forming accountable-care organizations, although other sectors are joining in.
SOURCE: Leavitt Partners.

as well as EHRs filled with the right data. Your doctor can only make the right decisions about your care if she has all of your health data—and in an ACO, she will.

This is where the payers (health insurance companies) step in. Since much of the data necessary to assess an ACOs performance may come from health claims—such as whether you've refilled your prescriptions or made it to all of your physical therapy appointments—it makes sense that payers are part of this picture.

Many payer-provider ACOs are already up and running. These include Aetna-Banner Health in Arizona; Blue Shield of California, Hoag Memorial Hospital Presbyterian, and Greater Newport Physicians; and Cigna-Granite Healthcare Network in New Hampshire. More are on the way. Experts who study ACOs say payers are natural partners and leaders in developing this new model of health care; insurers have a bottom-line interest in the outcome, they already have plenty of data, and may have more dollars at their disposal for buying the innovative IT needed to run them.[24]

This means payers will be funding health information technology (HIT) advances. HIT upgrades are sorely needed in order to make ACOs tick, say Harvard School of Public Health researchers in a 2011 *Journal of the American Medical Association* commentary called "Implementing Accountable Care Organizations: Ten Potential Mistakes and How to Learn From Them."[25] Among the gaps cited: underusing electronic records, not fully engaging patients in self-care, underreporting performance data, and not implementing standardized care practices. Are you listening, payers and tech innovators? You just read your to-do list for most-needed innovations—now it's your turn to deliver!

The Private Sector: Leveraging Technology, Filling Unmet Needs

By nature, I believe in permitting our capitalist system to work. It's at its best when vetting ideas and sorting out the real winners and losers. Government can only drive the healthcare IT revolution so far. Ours is one of the most innovative nations on Earth. Our private sector is capable of creating all the tools we will need to fix the healthcare industry. And, the healthcare industry will need to fix itself.

Entrepreneurs are emerging and capital is being invested in innovations aimed at improving our health system. We must make sure that an adequate reward system is in place for those who succeed. Ultimately, the savings gained through healthcare IT will pay for the system changes, but the line back to individual innovations will not always be direct. The experts need to be engaged with no limit to the potential for their inventions.

This means changing the short-term view, too prevalent in a healthcare industry that considers paying for innovation as only an expense. Instead, we need to extend our view to the horizon and embrace healthcare IT as an investment in more efficient and effective care for the future. We need to look beyond what a given innovation can do tomorrow for one group of patients and fix our vision on its capacity to influence the whole of health care for generations to come.

By targeting unmet needs, leveraging technology, and delivering enhanced value, the private sector is in a position to create transformative solutions that will change health care for the better—forever. Right now, American health care is like a heart patient in need of a bypass. Continuing with the way things are could prove fatal.

Enter private enterprise. With plenty of money on the table (investments in healthcare IT are expected to be one of the healthcare system's biggest growth areas in the coming years), industry should continue to lead the charge with innovative solutions. In my view, private industry can and should create innovations that go far beyond government's "meaningful use" mandates to create breathtaking new products and services.

Right now, there's plenty of room for innovation. Our system stills relies too heavily on paper—astonishing in a world where most of us rely on computers, laptops, tablets, and smartphones for everything from doing our jobs to writing out the grocery list to planning a vacation.

Think about health IT innovators, and big software companies may come to mind—companies like Epic Systems of Madison, Wisconsin, which handles the digital needs of major medical centers including Cedars-Sinai Medical Center in Los Angeles, the Cleveland Clinic, and

Johns Hopkins Medicine in Baltimore; integrated health systems like Kaiser Permanente; as well as medical groups like the Weill Cornell Physicians Organization in New York. But innovation comes in small, niche packages, too. Think about what every provider and every hospital must do when electronic records come in: Scan relevant information now scrawled in thousands upon thousands of paper files. That calls for bridge technology such as Digitech Systems, which helps providers move the right data into their records.

There's room for innovation in every corner of health care. Ahead in this book, I'll outline big growth areas for IT investors. For now, let's take a quick look at how and where innovation in health IT is happening in America.

Here are five examples of how private industry is creating innovative, digital solutions to fill unmet healthcare needs.

#1: **The smart health boom**: Smart health innovators are harnessing mobile apps, the Internet, social networking, and more to educate consumers, link people with good health information, and give scientists and health experts access to data about how people behave in the real world when it comes to managing their own health. Great examples of smart health innovations include SegTerra, which uses biomarkers uncovered in blood tests two to four times a year to help consumers establish informed, personal health goals. Another innovator, Anthurium Solutions, Inc., provides software that helps people with chronic health conditions find health professionals and coaches to help them manage their condition proactively.

#2: **Instant drug reference:** Thanks to Epocrates's drug-information program for mobile devices and tablets, your doctor can check on the right dosage, interactions, and side effects while the two of you talk during your appointment. At least 60 percent of practicing internists use the San Mateo, California, company's handy drug guide—and it's free. The company says the app prevents up to 16 million adverse drug events a year. Other mobile products from Epocrates include an anatomy app for med students and doctors who want their patients to really "get" what's happening inside the human body. Started by a pair of Stanford University students, Epocrates went public in 2011—an example of an innovative tech start-up succeeding by improving health care.

#3: **Healthcare IT incubator:** San Francisco-based Rock Health calls itself "the first seed accelerator for digital health start-ups." Bright minds with bright ideas can apply for a $20,000 start-up grant that comes with office space at headquarters or at Harvard Medical School in Cambridge, Massachusetts; support from experts at Harvard, the Mayo Clinic Center for Innovation, the University of California San Francisco, and Cincinnati Children's Hospital; mentoring from experts in law, finance, design, health policy, and more. While start-ups are usually kept in "stealth mode" during development, early start-ups that got help from Rock include CellScope for at-home disease diagnosis and Genomera for crowd-sourced health studies.

#4: **Deep wireless telehealth**: Sending blood pressure, blood sugar, and body weight measurements over the Internet to your doctor can keep you healthy and even save your life. But NeuroVigil took the concept to a whole new level with the iBrain headband, which captures brainwave data via wireless electrodes. The company's software turns data points into a new kind of sleep map that reveals never-before-seen details about sleep architecture. This breakthrough could help with early disease diagnosis (including early warnings of Parkinson's disease) and give us a new understanding of how medications affect the brain, allowing for better individualized disease treatments.

#5: The big competition: America spends an estimated $30 billion a year on unnecessary hospitalizations. Now, the Heritage Provider Network—a Northridge, California, physicians group that develops healthcare delivery networks—is offering a $3 million prize for the computer algorithm that can best identify patients likely to land in the hospital within the next year. The idea is that identifying at-risk patients gives them and their doctors time to make health changes that head off a trip to the local medical center. The prize is bigger than the Nobel Prize for Medicine and the Gates Health Prize, and has drawn 4,500 teams including physicists, mathematicians, computer scientists, and stochastic modelers (a method to estimate probability, sometimes used in financial markets). The winner of the world's biggest predictive modeling contest will be announced in 2013. "We have an opportunity to change the world," notes Heritage CEO Richard Merkin. "If we create an algorithm that helps society avoid unnecessary costly hospitalizations, we can take those savings and use them for research to find cures for costly diseases. Indeed, a solution to the Heritage Health Prize challenge can help solve the country's $2 trillion dollar healthcare crisis and save money for families who are currently spending $1 out of every $4 dollars of their budget on health care."[26]

Action by Government, Payers, and the Private Sector Needed to Succeed

Three players have key roles to play in the dramatic transformation of healthcare IT. It will require coordinated action by all three to see the transformation to its conclusion.

The federal government needs to do three things. It needs to start rewarding success instead of funding failure; to provide mandates, standards, and incentives for electronic health record systems and health information exchanges; and to provide seed money, as it did in the HITECH Act, the DIRECT program, and the Health Care Innovation Awards program.

Healthcare plans and insurers need to invest heavily in healthcare IT; specifically in EHRs, EMRs, and HIEs. Enter the EHR market. They also need to continue their exploration of accountable care organizations, in which primary-care doctors, specialists, and hospitals work together as a team to care for a group of patients and are held accountable for the cost and quality of that care.

The private sector needs to do what it does best: vetting ideas and sorting out the real winners and losers. Of course, we also must ensure that an adequate reward system is in place for those who succeed. And I am convinced we will succeed.

There are successful models out there in the world beyond our borders. We have a lot to learn from—and perhaps to teach—other countries, even those whose healthcare systems are notably different from ours. The next chapter takes a look at developments in Denmark, the Netherlands, and New Zealand.

Notes

1. IBM, "Making Sense of Medical Data," www.ibm.com/ibm/licensing/industry/healthcare/.

2. WellPoint, "Cedars-Sinai's Samuel Oschin Cancer Center Joins WellPoint in Developing Health Care Solutions," December 16, 2011, http://ir.wellpoint.com/phoenix.zhtml?c=130104&p=irol-newsArticle&ID=1640553&highlight=.

3. Tom Groenfeldt. "IBM's Watson, Cedars-Sinai and WellPoint Take On Cancer," *Forbes*, February 2, 2012.

4. Associated Press, "IBM's Watson Moving to Health Insurance," September 12, 2011, www.toledoblade.com/Technology/2011/09/12/IBM-s-Watson-moving-to-health-insurance.html.

5. E. S, Chen, G. B. Melton, and I. N. Sarkar, "Translating Standards into Practice: Experiences and Lessons Learned in Biomedicine and Health Care," *J Biomed Inform*, June 29, 2012..

6. The Direct Project, "The Direct Project Overview," http://wiki.directproject.org/file/view/DirectProjectOverview.pdf.

7. The Direct Project, "Implementation Group Committed Organizations," http://wiki.directproject.org/Implementation+Group+Committed+Organizations.

8. The Direct Project, "VisionShare," http://wiki.directproject.org/Pilot+Project+Brief+-+VisionShare+and+Public+Health.

9. The Direct Project, "Rhode Island Quality Institute," http://wiki.directproject.org/file/view/RIQI+-+Direct+Project+-+Simple+Consent+Architecture+-+vFINAL.pdf.

10. Trudi Matthews, "HealthBridge and Indiana Health Organizations Showcase Provider-Patient Information Sharing," HealthBridge, March 4, 2012, www.healthbridge.org/index.php?option=com_content&task=view&id=112&Itemid=2.

11. The Direct Project, http://directproject.org/content.php?key=pilots.

12. Chun-Ju Hsiao, Esther Hing, Thomas C. Socey, and Bill Cai, "Electronic Health Record Systems and Intent to Apply for Meaningful Use Incentives among Office-Based Physician Practices: United States, 2001–2011," CDC.

13. Dustin Charles, Michael Furukawa, and Meghan Hufstader, "Electronic Health Record Systems and Intent to Attest to Meaningful Use among Non-Federal Acute Care Hospitals in the United States: 2008–2011," ONC Data Brief no. 1, February 2012, www.healthit.gov/media/pdf/ONC_Data_Brief_AHA_2011.pdf.

14. U.S. Department of Health and Human Services Press Release, "HHS Announces 81 Health Care Innovation Awards," June 15, 2012, www.hhs.gov/news/press/2012pres/06/20120615a.html.

15. Centers for Medicare and Medicaid Services, "Health Care Innovation Awards: North Dakota," http://innovations.cms.gov/initiatives/Innovation-Awards/north-dakota.html.

16. Centers for Medicare and Medicaid Services, "Health Care Innovation Awards: Minnesota," http://innovations.cms.gov/initiatives/Innovation-Awards/minnesota.html.

17. Centers for Medicare and Medicaid Services, "Health Care Innovation Awards: Texas," http://innovations.cms.gov/initiatives/Innovation-Awards/texas.html.

18. NextGen Healthcare Press Release, "NextGen Healthcare Partners with Humana to Accelerate Adoption and Exchange of Electronic Health Records," February 15, 2012, www.nextgen.com/pdf/PR_Humana_12_2_15.pdf.

19. NaviNet Press Release, "Blues Plans, Lumeris Partner to Acquire Nation's Largest Real-Time Health Care Communication Network," February 14, 2012, www.navinet.net/about/press/acquisition-by-highmark-horizon-ibc-lumeris.

20. "UnitedHealthcare Donates $125,000 to Three Arizona Medical Facilities to Help Improve Health Care Delivery for Local Residents," *BusinessWire*, December 1, 2011, www.businesswire.com/news/home/20111201005117/en/UnitedHealthcare-Donates-125000-Arizona-Medical-Facilities-Improve.

21. Blue Cross Blue Shield of North Carolina News Release, "BCBSNC, Allscripts Announce New Program to Implement Electronic Health Records with More Than 750 North Carolina Physicians," September 28, 2011, http://mediacenter.bcbsnc.com/pr/bluecross/bcbsnc-allscripts-announce-new-216311.aspx.

22. Blue Cross Blue Shield of Michigan News Release, "Blue Cross Blue Shield of Michigan's Health Care Quality Efforts with Hospitals Save More Than $232 Million Statewide over Three-Year Period," April 17, 2012, http://news.bcbsm.com/news/2012/news_2012-04-17-15144.shtml.

23. Leavitt Partners, "Growth and Dispersion of Accountable Care Organizations,". http://news.leavittpartners.com/newsrelease-cid-1-id-43.html.

24. Victor R. Fuchs and Leonard D. Schaeffer, "If Accountable Care Organizations Are the Answer, Who Should Create Them?" *JAMA* 307, no. 21 (2012): 2261–2262, doi:10.1001/jama.2012.5564.

25. Sara Singer and Stephen M. Shortell, "Implementing Accountable Care Organizations: Ten Potential Mistakes and How to Learn From Them," *JAMA* 306, no. 7 (2011): 758–759, doi:10.1001/jama.2011.1180.

26. Heritage Provider Network Health Prize, "Improve Healthcare, Win $3,000,000," April 2011, www.heritagehealthprize.com/c/hhp.

Chapter 7

Global Healthcare IT

Three Case Studies

Depending on their philosophy, politicians and pundits often praise the American healthcare system as "the best in the world" or declare it "irretrievably broken." Stories about people waiting years for an elective surgery or about new mothers receiving free weekly visits from a home-health aide who even does the dishes have become the stuff of urban myth.

The truth is probably somewhere in between. Serious researchers and observers know that, however you describe it, our healthcare system can be improved. We can save more lives, work more efficiently and effectively, and improve the nation's overall well-being.

These three case studies from Denmark, the Netherlands, and New Zealand put the opportunities and challenges ahead of us in perspective.

Denmark: Fostering Digital Health Care

With over 10,000 beds and more than 65,000 outpatient visits per year, Thy-Mors Hospital in northern Denmark is a busy medical center. It's also on the cutting edge of healthcare IT. When doctors and other practitioners call up a patient's electronic health record, they see more than words and numbers: Up pops a three-dimensional image of the human body that can be rotated, enlarged, and even displays muscles, nerves, bones, and organs—all tied to details in a patient's record.[1]

But stunning graphics aren't the only way in which this small country—Denmark has about six million residents and is roughly the size of Wisconsin—is leading the way in digital health care. According to the nonprofit Commonwealth Fund, Denmark's deeply interconnected health information system is among the most efficient in the world.[2] Not only does it save doctors nearly an hour a day compared with the old days of paper record-keeping; a 2008 report from the Healthcare Information and Management Systems Society estimates that the country's digital changeover, begun in the 1990s, is saving the Danish health system up to $120 million a year.[3]

Danish citizens are reaping the benefits. They can access their health records online through sundhed.dk, a national healthcare portal that allows them to refill prescriptions, review their medical history, book doctor appointments, and e-mail practitioners—and expect a reply. Use of e-mail by doctors has been mandatory since 2009—and physicians are paid twice as much for communicating via the Internet with their patients as they are for phone consultations. New tele-health projects are bringing advanced home care to people with a common breathing disorder called chronic obstructive pulmonary disease, to people with dangerous diabetic foot ulcers (a major risk factor for amputations), and heart patients with off-beat heart rhythms.

No wonder Danes have the highest rates of satisfaction with their healthcare system in the European Union.[4] Here's how it developed, along with a look at the unique factors behind Denmark's HIT success and a glimpse at where this system is headed in the future.

HIT Foundation

Frustrated with rising healthcare administrative costs and ready to move beyond regional attempts at electronic medical record-keeping, Denmark established MedCom—its coordinating organization for healthcare IT—in 1994. Funded by the National Ministry of Health and by local government, among other groups, MedCom set out to establish standards for six key areas of digital health: Lab orders and results; prescriptions ordered by general practitioners; referrals to specialists; radiology orders and results; community (home care) messages; and insurance claims submissions and reimbursements. At first, the standards were sent out to local health IT projects funded locally by Denmark's counties. The government mandated the adoption of EMRs by all primary care physicians by 2004—and provided incentives like faster reimbursements for participating doctors and the equivalent of 1,500 euros a year for practitioners to spend on electronic health records.

It worked. Today, 100 percent of Denmark's primary-care physicians have gone digital. Most medical communication between primary care doctors, specialists, and hospitals is electronic. According to a 2010 Commonwealth Fund report, the Danish Health Data Network transmits 3.5 million messages per month. The network transmits approximately 100 percent of discharge letters, 95 percent of lab results, 80 percent of reimbursements, 77 percent of prescriptions, 52 percent of referrals, and 15 percent of lab requests.[5]

Every Danish citizen has his or her own national identification number that helps keep medical records coordinated and accessible. Healthcare professionals need a patient's consent to view the record.

Factors behind Denmark's Success

A computer-savvy citizenry, high trust in government, and a history of a centralized, national patient registry dating to the 1970s all helped. It didn't hurt that Denmark is a small country with a healthcare system already run by the public sector. MedCom worked closely with healthcare practitioners to establish standards, which created precise, usable, accurate medical communication standards—and a buy-in from practitioners. Financial incentives, the acceptance that adopting electronic records would take years, and freedom for practitioners to choose their own systems from vendors enhanced adoption rates. It's interesting to note that MedCom also fostered friendly competition by posting on its website the number of health-related messages sent electronically in each county, and the progress of vendors toward compliance with the standards.

"What we found is that EHR adoption must be done by evolution rather than revolution," Jens Andersen of sundhed. dk, the state healthcare Web portal, told *Time* magazine in 2009. "You have to work with the systems already in place."[6]

Bumps in the Road

No system is perfect. As of 2010, many patient visits to the doctor in Denmark are still not coded into electronic health records. This gap makes analyzing performance and outcomes more difficult and means researchers don't have as much data for large studies. And an early coding system was considered too complex for doctors and nurses to use, and was abandoned in 2006; physicians use a variety of record-keeping systems that are linked.

Ahead for Denmark

The nation's largest-ever telemedicine project got under way in 2012 with about 2,000 patients with a wide variety of health needs.

"There is no doubt that it is the way we should go. Patients are saved the trouble of going to hospital, and hospital beds are saved," Health Minister Astrid Krag said recently about Denmark's telemedicine push. "With close telemedical supervision the professional hospital staff can detect early if the condition is worsening in a patient in their living room. It can prevent costly hospitalizations."[7]

Innovative telehealth pilot projects under way in Denmark involve home monitoring of patients with a variety of health conditions including heart disease, a breathing problem called chronic obstructive pulmonary disease (COPD), diabetes, and inflammatory bowel diseases; as well as pregnant women with and without complications. Here are details on three:

- **Monitoring breathing problems at home**. People with COPD will receive home care from trained caregivers who will transmit their vital signs to the hospital.[8]

- **Tracking diabetic foot ulcers**. Foot wounds are common in people with diabetes, and can lead to amputation. In this program, visiting nurses will photograph foot ulcers of people with diabetes at home. Hospital-based experts will review the photos and make recommendations.[9]
- **Measuring heart rhythms**. Heart patients will wear ePatches for remote monitoring of cardiac arrhythmias that can lead to heart attacks.[10]

The Netherlands: A Controversy over National Health Records

Health informatics experts date the start of the Netherlands' relationship with electronic medical records to 1978, when the first Dutch family doctor reportedly set up a computer in his office. By 1983, 35 pioneering physicians had gone digital, according to Denis Prossi, a digital health professor from the University of Victoria in Canada. And by 2010, 99 percent of practitioners in this nation beside the North Sea were using some form of electronic medical records. That high adoption rate has made the Netherlands a leader in healthcare IT, a fact widely reported by the American media and by healthcare think tanks when our own government began taking steps to bring our healthcare system into the digital age with the HITECH Act in 2009.

But there's a surprising twist to the Netherlands health IT story that's gotten little attention in the United States.

Yes, digital health records are the norm in this nation of 16 million people. And doctors, hospitals, pharmacies, and labs exchange health data electronically on a local and regional level. But the Dutch government's effort to take the system to the next level—by linking local health records via a nationwide system with wider access for providers—failed dramatically in 2010. Citing security and privacy worries, the Dutch senate unanimously rejected Health Minister Edith Schippers' plan to introduce a nationwide Electronic Patient Dossier (EPD) in the Netherlands, ending a plan that had been 14 years in the making and had cost the government 217 million euros.

What went wrong? The Dutch EPD system would *not* have created national health records for each citizen. Instead, records already kept locally by family doctors—plus additional data stored by pharmacies, specialists, and hospitals—would be summarized and available to providers throughout the country. Connections would be provided by a National Switching Point (LSP in Dutch), which would have functioned like a health-record search engine. In fact, the LSP was described at the time as a "Google for health care." The LPS was designed to store references to patient records, organized by an ID number, for each Dutch resident. Authorized users like doctors, pharmacists, and hospital staff would have access to parts or all of the record. Unauthorized users would be kept out because they would not have the coded passwords and key cards needed to enter the system.

Up to 60 percent of Dutch providers had voluntarily joined this system, linking up the medical records of over 5 million Dutch citizens, when opposition to the plan led Dutch politicians to call a halt in early 2010. Leading the charge against it were family-doctor groups—one called *Comité WAKE UP!!*—who opposed the top-down rules imposed by government. They cited security worries, worries that patient records would be incomplete or misinterpreted, and concerns that maintaining patient records under the new system would impose a financial and scheduling burden on family doctors. One survey of doctors found that 30 percent opposed the plan and another 25 percent considered lodging an objection.[11]

Dutch citizens were apparently worried, too. In 2008, the government mailed a brochure to every household in the country, describing the upcoming system and announcing deadlines for commenting on the plan. Within seven weeks, 330,000 people objected. By March of 2009, over 400,000 people registered their opposition.

Why did the same physicians who had once pioneered electronic medical records in their own practices and used them daily put their foot down when it came to linking a national system—despite the health gains and cost savings already documented in neighboring European countries? To find out, researchers from the Netherlands Institute for Health Services Research conducted in-depth interviews with doctors working in acute care, diabetes care, and ambulatory mental health care.[12] Here's what they learned about why the national system failed:

- **Safety concerns**: The researchers found that physicians were worried that unauthorized persons "would have access to electronic patient data, either because people could hack the system, or as a result of healthcare providers' carelessness (e.g., leaving their computer screen unattended or using insecure e-mail connections to exchange patient information)." Doctors also worried that their colleagues might abuse the system by browsing the records of other patients. "If someone succeeds in breaking into the National Switch Point, I'm afraid that it'll be over. That's my biggest fear, that there'll be leaks or that people will be careless," one noted.
- **Incomplete records:** Doctors were concerned that health records wouldn't give a full picture of patients'

health, for several reasons. Some noted that not all physicians coded data from patient visits, instead recording them as free text that might not be accessible to other providers. "If an episode is titled 'finger' or 'knee,' you still don't know what's wrong," one physician said.

- **Privacy issues:** Other doctors said they would be less candid in recording future data, to protect patients' privacy. "My recording of patient information will definitely change if others will have access to my patient records. Information about personality disorders and violence or rape, with names and all, will just be left out," one noted.[13]

Despite the reluctance of many in the Netherlands to link their HIT system on a national level, clinicians and researchers are making significant use of regionally-available health records to analyze important healthcare issues. Recently published research arising from Dutch data includes these four insightful studies:

- **Quality checks for midwives.** Three out of four pregnant women in the Netherlands start their maternity care with one of the country's over 24,000 midwives. One in three has a midwife-attended birth. Researchers at Amsterdam's Vrije Universiteit Medical Center have begun compiling a database that will track the quality of midwifery care from preconception to postbirth. They published a paper on their methods in 2012; continuing analysis will be the foundation for evidence-based maternity care.[14]
- **Mental health care for kids and teens.** Working with more than 37,000 patient records, researchers from the Netherlands Institute for Health Services Research recently examined early treatment of children and teens with mental health issues.[15] They found that the system is identifying kids who need help, and many might be

helped by family doctors instead of being referred to specialists.

- **Lifestyle changes for people with diabetes and pre-diabetes**. As more and more people are at risk for diabetes, the importance of identifying powerful, preventive steps grows. In a study from Maastricht University, researchers tracked over 2,800 people with prediabetes and diabetes to see whether lifestyle changes worked as well, or better, than usual care with medications for blood sugar, high cholesterol, and high blood pressure. Both groups saw improvements.[16]

- **The quality of after-hours health care**. If you have to take a spouse, child, or yourself to an after-hours clinic for a minor health emergency, will your care be as good as going to your own doctor during the day? Radboud University researchers checked the records of 7,660 after-hours clinic visits to see if patient care met guidelines (such as proper prescribing of pain relievers and antibiotics, and proper referral to specialists). They rated care as good: It met guidelines 77 percent of the time, though antibiotics were often over- or underprescribed.[17]

New Zealand: Interoperability Leader

In New Zealand, the use of health information technology is wide and deep. All of the nation's approximately 1,100 general-medicine practices use an electronic medical record system. And they're well-connected. Family doctors, specialists, hospitals, radiologists, and medical labs use standard messaging to communicate with each other. An estimated 50 million separate pieces of clinical and administrative information are exchanged annually, putting New Zealand at the forefront of interoperability.

General practitioners' systems perform many functions, with the capacity to:

- Print medication prescriptions.
- Manage medication lists.
- Receive alerts for potential adverse drug interactions.
- Generate problem lists.
- Enter clinical progress notes.
- Perform clinical messaging.
- Issue automatic preventive reminders.
- Access external decision-support programs.
- Access patients' medical records from outside the office.
- Receive rapid automated status messages (detailing hospital visits or admissions, receipt of referrals, or other clinical updates) and electronic discharge summaries for each patient.
- Communicate with national registries (e.g., immunization databases) and report quality indicators electronically.

Easing into Healthcare IT

It's interesting to note that by the early 1990s, early electronic medical records vendors and health IT companies in New Zealand were developing digital decision-support and chronic-disease care systems for the nation's doctors. At the same time, New Zealand's government in 1992 introduced an advance that helped pave the way for a national system: National Health Index (NHI) numbers. Every patient received one; the number was used for health insurance claims, referrals, lab tests, and prescriptions.

These developments, along with a new health-information privacy code that requires patient approval for providers to share information, paved the way. Even before the arrival of the Internet, private communications networks in New Zealand—called "value added networks"—helped doctors share information. One, HealthLink, helped facilitate information exchanges between primary-care doctors, specialists, and hospitals. One important landmark: New Zealand was the first country in the world to widely use HL7-based messaging—an internationally recognized standard—for the reporting of lab test results and radiology data and for specialist referrals and hospital discharge reports, for delivery of pathology and radiology information to general practices, and for referrals and discharge summaries on a widespread basis.

Government encouraged doctors to adopt technology, too. In 1998, family-medicine practices in several regions received a grant equal to about $3,600 in U.S. dollars to buy computers—and told family doctors they would be required to file health-insurance claims electronically within two years. By 2000, more than 98 percent had digital billing and appointments systems; over half used IT to maintain electronic patient records. Government also pushed doctors to leverage digital health information to improve the nation's health, by requiring them to send some patient information to national registries. One, a national child immunization registry, was developed in 2000 after a meningitis outbreak. Other registries track diabetes management and screenings for hepatitis B.

The new rules came with incentives to adopt new software, as well as funding for IT vendors to develop interfaces to connect systems. The result: A rich, deeply interoperable system.

A "Distributed" Approach

And yet, as a 2010 Commonwealth Fund report on New Zealand's health IT system notes, the country "takes a very conservative approach to the sharing of personal health information." Patient records are kept by your family doctor, not in a central data bank. A robust communications system (as of 2010, 80 percent of family doctors' systems could handle real-time messaging) means quick, efficient communication using standard Internet connections or a secure private network.

Nearly all clinical communication is electronic. Among the benefits:

- **Information, fast**. Data from a hospital visit, specialist appointment, or after-hours clinic for a minor medical emergency is usually incorporated into a patient's electronic medical record within just two hours.
- **Care reminders**. Over 90 percent of New Zealanders receive reminder notices when they're due for regular or follow-up care (in most other countries, just 3 to 48 percent get reminders). And 96 percent of doctors keep lists of patients who are due, or past due, for tests or preventive care.
- **Fast prescription–drug approvals**. The New Zealand government strictly controls which prescription drugs it covers. Getting approval for an off-list medication used to require sending faxes, mailing forms, and waiting for more than a week. Now doctors using an online approval system can get authorization in just 20 seconds.[18]

Global Lessons Hold Domestic Value

Every culture is different. There are social norms guiding attitudes about data-sharing and the delivery of health care. Citizens are more or less technically inclined, carrying potentially more or less trust of technology-enabled health care. Every government system drives an ecosystem of contextual incentives and barriers. We are different across the globe. And yet, more and more, we realize how much we are the same and how much we can learn from each other. There are rich lessons to be learned from the systems of other countries. We don't have to adopt those systems wholesale, but we can learn what is driving success in areas where we in the United States are struggling.

And why wouldn't we? The bottom line is that we spend significantly more in the United States on health care, and we get significantly less for our money in terms of health outcomes. Broader adoption of technology and the accessibility of information across providers and by patients holds great potential as a catalyst for change.

The vast amounts of data that the healthcare IT transformation promises to deliver could easily overwhelm us if not properly stored, analyzed, and deployed. In the next chapter, I take a look at how some other industries are mining their data for profit and competitive advantage, and how those techniques might be used in the healthcare industry by a new kind of health data analyst.

Notes

1. IBM Press Release, "IBM and Danish Hospital Pioneer Smarter Patient Records to Improve Patient Care," March 10, 2009, http://www-03.ibm.com/press/us/en/pressrelease/26870.wss.

2. Denis Protti, "Widespread Adoption of Information Technology in Primary Care Physician Offices in Denmark: A Case Study," Issues in International Health Policy, The Commonwealth Fund, March 2010, www.commonwealthfund.org/~/media/Files/Publications/Issue%20Brief/2010/Mar/1379_Protti_widespread_adoption_IT_primary_care_Denmark_intl_ib.pdf.

3. "Electronic Health Records: A Global Perspective," HIMSS Enterprise Systems Steering Committee and the Global Enterprise

Task Force, August 2008, www.himss.org/content/files/200808_ehrglobalperspective_whitepaper.pdf.

4. Protti, "Widespread Adoption of Information Technology."

5. Jonathan Edwards, "Case Study: Denmark's Achievements with Healthcare Information Exchange," Gartner Industry Research, May 30, 2006.

6. Eben Harrell, "In Denmark's Electronic Health Records Program, a Lesson for the U.S.," *Time*, April 16, 2009, www.time.com/time/health/article/0,8599,1891209,00.html#ixzz21PhaCdfA.

7. "DK: Largest-Ever Telemedicine Project Launched," ePractice.eu, January 17, 2012, www.epractice.eu/en/news/5324811.

8. Birthe Dinesen, "Development of a Program for Tele-Rehabilitation of COPD Patients across Sectors: Co-Innovation in a Network," *International Journal of Integrated Care* 29, March 2011, www.ijic.org/index.php/ijic/article/viewArticle/582/1234.

9. "Project Tele Ulcer Care," ePractice.eu, January 29, 2011, www.epractice.eu/en/cases/teleulcercare.

10. "Denmark, England and Scotland Are at the Forefront of Telehealth... Rethinking Healthcare," European Commision: Europe's Information Society, Thematic Portal, http://ec.europa.eu/information_society/newsroom/cf/itemdetail.cfm?item_id=8071.

11. Stephen Verhage, "Better Health Care through Better Information? Mapping the Health Care Information Technology of the EPD and the Controversy over Its Implementation in Dutch Health Care," http://devrijehuisarts.org/stukkenpdf/ThesisEPDStephenVerhage.pdf.

12. Marieke Zwaanswijk, Robert A. Verheij, Floris J. Wiesman, and Roland D. Friele, "Benefits and Problems of Electronic Information Exchange as Perceived by Health Care Professionals: An Interview Study," *BMC Health Services Research* 11, 2011: 256, www.biomed-central.com/1472-6963/11/256.

13. Ibid.

14. Judith Manniën, "Evaluation of Primary Care Midwifery in the Netherlands: Design and Rationale of a Dynamic Cohort Study (DELIVER)," *BMC Health Services Research* 12, 2012: 69.

15. M. Zwaanswijk, "Child and Adolescent Mental Health Care in Dutch General Practice: Time Trend Analyses," *BMC Fam Pract* 12, December 2011: 133.

16. J. J. Linmans, "Effect of Lifestyle Intervention for People with Diabetes or Prediabetes in Real-World Primary Care: Propensity Score Analysis," *BMC Fam Pract* 12, September 2011: 95.

17. M. Willekens, "Quality of After-Hours Primary Care in the Netherlands: Adherence to National Guidelines," *BMJ Qual Saf* 20, no. 3 (March 2011:223–227.

18. Denis Protti, "Electronic Medical Record Adoption in New Zealand Primary Care Physician Offices," Issues in International Health Policy, The Commonwealth Fund, August 2010.

Chapter 8

Real-Time Learning

Instant Data Mining and Medical Breakthroughs

Hotel chains, delivery firms, and insurance companies are today as well known for their sophisticated use of data mining and analytics as they are for their core businesses. The analysts at Marriott International honed their skills on establishing the optimal price for a hotel room in any given market. Over time, the company has even created a "revenue opportunity model, which computes actual revenues as a percentage of the optimal rates that could have been charged. That figure has grown from 83 percent to 91 percent as Marriott's revenue-management analytics have taken root."[1]

UPS tracks more than your packages: It puts its extensive databases to use anticipating which customers are most likely to defect to one of its competitors. When a waffling customer is identified, a salesperson goes to work to identify and resolve the issues that are causing dissatisfaction.[2]

Progressive Insurance uses not only its own data, but more widely available insurance industry data to define groups of consumers within very specific parameters. More specific than the typical age, sex, and geography categories, Progressive delves into factors such as education levels and credit scores. Using regression and other analyses, analysts correlate specific factors with insurance losses, all to help Progressive set prices. The company goes a step further and uses simulation software to test its hypotheses. The result: Instead of rejecting high-risk applicants out of hand, Progressive is able to insure them at a profit.[3]

Advances in technology have brought an explosion of cutting-edge tools for analyzing vast pools of real-time data, and this capacity for on-the-fly data analysis is changing the face of whole industries, from casinos to retail giants to the financial sector. Forward-thinking companies have adapted to the era of real-time data by learning to assimilate more information and use it to make decisions more rapidly than ever before. Companies who were early adopters of these tools have seen their boldness pay off in increased profits.

What do the achievements of Marriott, UPS, or Progressive have to do with health care? Imagine that, rather than predicting which customer was about to switch from UPS to DHL, analysts instead mined data on which hospital patients were most likely to carry life-threatening infections. This isn't a futuristic scenario—it's already happening at NorthShore University HealthSystem Illinois. Using electronic medical records data, the organization has adopted a method of predictive modeling that's enabled them to target their screening for methicillin-resistant *Staphylococcus aureus* (MRSA) infections. The system works—it has allowed NorthShore to successfully identify 99 percent of its MRSA carriers by testing just half of all patients.

Plenty of firms use data analytics to improve their profitability. The payoffs are even greater in the healthcare industry, where the stakes are not just money, but lives. When we apply real-time data analysis to the medical system, the results are enormous—healthier citizens living longer, more productive lives, all because a few pioneers made investments in computers, electronic medical records, and the people with skills to analyze the data.

Lives saved is a sufficient measure for most of us. But also consider the cost of illness in the United States. These real-time analytics have the potential to flatten the cost curve of our overall health system, saving tens of billions of dollars each year. The savings could help us to enhance other sectors of the economy by deploying that capital in a productive way. Even if all we did was reinvest this money into technology innovations focused on achieving better health for all, the pace of discovery would accelerate many times. We have the means to improve health while reducing cost. A win-win.

Introducing Real-Time Analytic Systems

The advent of electronic medical records and health information exchanges means that we now have the power to collect enormous amounts of medical data and make it instantly accessible across large geographical ranges, with profound implications. These data-pooling systems allow researchers to mine real-time medical statistics for insights that could lead to remarkable improvements in medical care. For instance, NorthShore mined its data on body temperature for post-operative patients and found that the norm for these patients is 100.3F—1.8 degrees warmer than for other hospital patients. Under most circumstances, a temperature above 98.5F indicates a cause for concern, but by raising this bar to 100.3F for post-op patients, NorthShore was able to significantly cut antibiotic use— reducing patient exposure to unnecessary side effects.

Still not convinced? Here are some examples of how Kaiser Permanente has achieved better health outcomes with data. In Colorado, we used data from our HealthConnect system to identify patients at risk for hypertension. They were personally contacted by care teams and received treatment in a dedicated hypertension clinic with frequent follow-up by care team members. After two years, we had increased by 16 percent the number of patients who were able to control their blood pressure.

We had similar success with a program to improve care for patients with diabetes in Ohio. This program supplemented HealthConnect data with daily data downloads for physicians from our pharmacy, lab, and radiology systems. This targeted approach generated significantly better outcomes: The percentage of patients with poor hemoglobin A1C control dropped from 41 percent to 21 percent; eye exams in this at-risk population increased from 52 percent to 75 percent; and hospital admissions were cut roughly in half.

The potential for data-mining to improve the way we deliver health care is enormous, and I predict that the impact on human health could equal that of vaccines. Physicians are trained to gauge and interpret their patients' symptoms to develop diagnoses and prognoses, but this process is susceptible to human error. Statistical algorithms can weigh and interpret medical data much faster and with greater consistency than the human mind. I'm not suggesting that data analytic systems can replace the physician's experience and judgment, but they can supplement them and provide a system for ensuring that medical decision-making is based on the best available evidence.

We know that it is almost impossible for already overworked physicians to do this kind of data analysis on an individual basis during patient visits. It would have taken extraordinary perceptiveness for NorthShore physicians to detect the body temperature differences among post-op patients that the organization's data analytic system identified so rapidly. Just imagine how many other new insights are awaiting discovery within the pools of data now becoming available. When a patient presents with complex symptoms and comorbidities, algorithms developed using instantaneous data sets could help physicians navigate the elaborate web of treatment possibilities. At the same time, real-time data collection allows doctors to feed individual patient treatment and outcome data back into the system, ensuring that patterns and correlations too opaque to catch an individual physician's eye will be detected and solutions implemented to improve patient care.

This new paradigm will rely on a comprehensive database connecting all points of the healthcare system—primary care, specialists, hospitals, laboratory, and pharmacy. As such databases come online, researchers and data analysts will have the ability to link outcomes to treatments and preventative care, monitor for adverse drug events, and conduct comparative effectiveness research in real time.

Medicine's New Superstar—The Health Data Analyst

Real-time data analytic systems depend on a new breed of healthcare worker—the health data analyst. These data jockeys turn patient records and medical databases into useful statistical information that can inform medical decision-making. In the age of real-time health care, medical data will pile up at an astounding rate, and it's the health data analyst's mission to turn these fast-accumulating data points into knowledge.

In the age of big data, workers with the training and skills to interpret data sets will become highly sought after. Google's chief economist, Hal Varian, told the *Economist* magazine in 2010 that "the job of statistician will become the 'sexiest' around."[4] Data, Varian told the *Economist*, are easy to come by, "what's scarce is the ability to extract wisdom from them."

Most health data analysts will have prior training or experience in the healthcare field, and will be familiar with medical terminology and basic medicine. They will have aptitudes for conceptual problem-solving and quantitative analysis and the ability to quickly absorb and learn new software applications. They might be assigned to monitor outcome data for a particular disease or patient population, or they may be tasked with tracking trends in the usage of specific types of interventions or services billed. Their work will inform healthcare organizations as they make decisions and determine guidelines and best practices. Hospitals, healthcare systems, and insurance companies are just some of the organizations that will rely on data analysts to improve their results and reduce costs.

Training data analysts could prove challenging, but the potential financial rewards are vast. A report, "Big Data: The Next Frontier for Innovation, Competition and Productivity," published by the McKinsey Global Institute[5] in 2011, estimates that data analysis could add $300 million worth of value to the American healthcare system each year. But the same report projected that for industries to realize the potential from data analysis, they'll need to find an additional 140,000 to 190,000 new workers with highly developed data analysis skills. Not only that, but the McKinsey report predicts that the United States will require another 1.5 million data-literate managers to work with these new data jockeys.

As this area becomes more sophisticated, the need for a new medical specialty will emerge. In addition to turning out doctors and nurses, medical colleges will need to partner with their mathematics departments to develop the coursework necessary to turn out sufficient numbers of people trained in this new specialty: medical data analyst. These people will be highly trained, highly skilled, and in demand right from college. As this area emerges, the knowledge we will gain as an industry or provider organization will not be limited to analyzing the information found strictly in medical records systems. These professionals will also be called on to correlate health outcomes associated with smartphones and their use by specific classes of patients. A vast array of data from a limitless possibility of sources will be gathered and analyzed, leading to advanced understanding of conditions as well as behavior—and the impact of both on health.

Care Registries: Putting Data into Practice

One way we've implemented data analysis at Kaiser Permanente is through our care registries, which track so-called high-priority patients to identify simple care gaps. Did a patient miss a doctor's appointment? Did the patient neglect to follow through on the lab work requested? Fail to renew a prescription on time? In any of these cases, the patient will receive an e-mail and perhaps even a phone call.

If the patient fails to follow up, their physician, rather than an administrator, may call them to make a personal connection and attempt to better understand the underlying issue or problem.

Such routine follow-up may sound like a no-brainer, yet it's rarely done in most medical practices today. Think back to the last time you missed a doctor's appointment or forgot to renew a prescription. Did anyone call? Was anyone there to check up on you? Did you feel cared for? Until now, if you're not a Kaiser Permanente member, the standard of care has been to place the responsibility for follow-up and routine care squarely on the patient. Yet it's clear that simple, proactive monitoring of care gaps like a missed appointment or a lapsed prescription can lead to better outcomes for patients.

At Kaiser Permanente Colorado, computer-supported cardiac care registries and a support program called the Collaborative Cardiac Care Service reduced overall mortality by 76 percent and deaths related to heart events by 73 percent among more than 12,000 patients with coronary artery disease, a leading cause of death and one of the top five chronic conditions driving the cost of medical care in the United States. The availability of electronic health data and instant access to patient information greatly enhanced the ability of clinical care teams to coordinate their efforts in cardiac care. All patient healthcare providers—from primary care physicians to pharmacists and physical therapists—have immediate access to reliable, evidence-based information they can use to support and monitor treatment adherence in a wide variety of settings. The innovative program has resulted in healthier people, which in turn saves money and resources, because healthy people don't show up at emergency rooms. We estimate that the program has prevented 135 deaths and 260 expensive emergency interventions each year.

Patient care registries can also help us conduct real-time safety and clinical effectiveness research. For instance, the Kaiser Permanente total joint replacement registry (TJRR) is tracking patient data on more than 100,000 joint replacement procedures. The program has five aims. First, to monitor revision, failure, and rates of complications; second, to identify patients most at risk for poor outcomes from total joint replacement procedures; third, to identify best practices and the most effective implant devices and techniques; fourth, to track implant usage statistics and cost; and finally, to support and monitor implant advisories or recalls from the U.S. Food and Drug Administration. The TJRR meets these goals by providing a way to aggregate and track real-time data on patients who have undergone total joint replacement.

Putting It All Together

Algorithms managed by health data analysts will scour the health IT systems in real time, looking for opportunities to detect potential problems before they become life threatening. With your permission, your insurer's database might link to the buyer's club card at your local grocery store, and if the system detects a sudden uptick in soft drink purchases, you might receive a text message or e-mail encouraging you to cut down your consumption of sugary beverages. Likewise, if your doctor has prescribed regular exercise for you, the system might provide gentle nudges, in the form of text messages or phone calls, to remind you to get out for your daily walk. Your physician may prescribe a smartphone app that helps you track your exercise and report back to the doctor's office, to give you extra incentive and support to meet your goals. When your physician's system detects that your prescription needs filling, you might get a digital reminder at just the right time.

These systems will help patients make better choices, but they'll also allow medical practice to reach its potential. Physicians who went to medical school hoping to improve people's health will finally be able to do what they aspired to: provide better health for many of their patients on a proactive basis, rather than only care for their patients after they become ill.

Imagine the patient who is expecting her second child. She's a busy, working mom. She wakes up in the morning and checks her computer to find a reminder of her doctor's appointment. She reaches for her mobile device and because she's in her second trimester and has been purchasing coffee at the grocery store frequently, her mobile health advisor reminds her of the optimum diet for this time in her pregnancy: less caffeine and more spinach, oranges, or beans to supplement her folic acid, according to Kaiser Permanente's expert doctors. It also reminds her to take her prenatal vitamin. She's grateful because she's never been one to remember daily medication.

She wears a wristband that takes her blood pressure every morning and sends the information to her doctor at the same time it tells her all is well. The band also checks her blood glucose levels. It shows the levels and recommends a list of carbohydrates that are options to bring her blood sugar level into balance, like brown rice or quinoa, and a variety of fruit. She drinks her orange juice and grabs an apple on her way out of the house. As she pulls out of the driveway, she notices a new mole on her neck in the rearview mirror. At work, she takes a picture of it with her webcam and e-mails it to her primary care physician. This starts in motion a collaborative approach to care, as the primary care physician sends the image for consultation with a dermatologist. The dermatologist views it on her tablet between visits at a downtown clinic, easily rotating the 3D view to get the full picture.

The patient gets a message from the dermatologist, "Come by after your 4:00 P.M. OB/GYN appointment."

In the dermatologist's office, just steps from her ob-gyn, the mole is examined and scanned by an IR/UV biopsy device. The doctor confirms what the readout says: "Condition is benign." She is relieved and is only thinking of getting home to her husband to let him know that all is well.

As she leaves the medical facility, she receives an SMS alert thanking her for her visit, and reminding her that her prenatal vitamin prescription refill is ready at the pharmacy. One less trip she'll have to squeeze in to her busy schedule later, and fewer days she'll go without her vitamin between prescriptions.

Does this sound impossible to you? It is a healthcare future that is within our grasp, and in practice today at Kaiser Permanente in many ways. As technologies increasingly converge, this and more will become commonplace. We are on the cusp of some of the greatest changes to our healthcare system in modern times. And everyone will be the beneficiary because the technology also will become more and more affordable over time, making these advances available even to those who have very modest means.

One of the most powerful changes may be a newfound capacity to move health care more firmly into the realms of preventive, and even predictive, medicine. Data, math, and science will soon give us the ability to find out what diseases we may be prone to. And innovations such as care registries are already having profound effects on our ability to improve the well-being of large populations at risk for chronic conditions like diabetes, hypertension, and asthma.

Notes

1. T. Davenport, "Competing on Analytics," *Harvard Business Review*, January 1, 2006, http://hbr.org/product/competing-on-analytics/an/R0601H-PDF-ENG.

2. Ibid.

3. Ibid.

4. "Data, Data Everywhere," *Economist*, February 25, 2010, www.economist.com/node/15557443.

5. James Manyika, Michael Chui, Brad Brown et al., "Big Data: The Next Frontier for Innovation, Competition, and Productivity," published by the McKinsey Global Institute, May 2011, www.mckinsey.com/insights/mgi.aspx.

Chapter 9

Predictive Medicine

Saving Time, Money, and Lives

Healthcare IT has come a very long way. Our methods have advanced to the point where we can use our data files, do some analysis, and help those with chronic disease have substantially better outcomes. That's preventive care. We can intervene, backed by emerging patterns in the data, to ensure the best possible health for our patients.

Consider this real-life example of preventive care at work.

A mammogram reminder in an improbable place— flashing on her allergist's computer screen—"saved my life" says Mary Gonzales. Hay fever, sniffles, and watery eyes brought this Southern California woman into a specialist's office one September morning. But her electronic medical record revealed something else: She was nearly two years overdue for a breast check.

"The receptionist said she wouldn't let me go without scheduling a mammogram," Gonzales recalls. "I'm really glad she pushed me. I would have waited a few more months on my own." The receptionist scheduled the mammogram immediately—and the test found a tiny, early-stage tumor. After surgery and radiation, Gonzales is cancer free today.[1]

Across the nation and around the world, real-time health care like this is taking medicine beyond "sick care" and putting the focus where it has always belonged: on keeping people healthy. We've only just begun. Fifty-seven percent of doctors and 18 percent of hospitals have made the leap from black bag–era, manila-folder health records to basic digitized electronic systems. Fewer have truly integrated electronic health systems. But those who have are already reporting powerful preventive-care outcomes:

- In the high rises on New York City's Roosevelt Island, internist Jack Resnick, MD, makes regular house calls on 50 homebound senior citizens—calling up their medical records on his ever-present laptop. Digitized health information, Resnick says, helps his oldest and frailest patients live at home longer and avoid unnecessary hospital and nursing home stays.[2]
- Data-checking software at Central Maine Medical Center flagged 65-year-old Ron Towle's high risk for an aortic aneurysm, a weak spot in the massive artery that feeds blood from the heart to the body. Ruptured aortic aneurysms kill 15,000 Americans each year. Towle's was caught in time and fixed before it could burst.[3]
- At Iowa's Cherokee Mental Health Institute, a computerized warning system helps staff avoid dangerous mix-ups

between drugs with look-alike and sound-alike names—a problem responsible for over a quarter-million drug errors each year in the United States.[4] In all, 1.5 million preventable drug errors happen each year in the nation, killing 100,000.[5] Studies show that moving to electronic medical records and installing electronic prescribing software would reduce them by 55 percent.[6]

But what technology also allows us to do is consider the potential for health. Our computers have the power to analyze even more data from sources we may not have ever considered in the past, and use that data to discover the potential for health problems and the opportunities we have to address them or avoid them altogether. What will soon be within our grasp is the ability to use data coupled with math and science to discover what diseases we may be prone to. Beyond risk factors that physicians use today to help patients manage their own health, we will be able to predict what illnesses patients will develop during their lifetimes. That kind of information can help us chart a path to avoid that illness. It may take us many years to fully uncover the potential that these new electronic databases carry, but the potential to further improve people's lives is a powerful driver.

It seems to us that if a few organizations can get substantial patient benefits from their use of information technology, widespread adoption holds broad hope that this transition to preventive care can save lives and make health care more affordable for everyone. I believe every patient in the United States and around the world should expect nothing less.

Will we save money? Yes; although calculating the amount may be difficult at first. After all, prevention and preventive care can't be patented or protected the way a blockbuster drug or the design for a new high-tech MRI scanner can be. Health isn't a profit center in that way. But it makes sense that preventing disease and controlling chronic health conditions is far more cost-effective than the neglect happening throughout our country's system now. As people get and stay healthier, they will be more productive on the job, more satisfied in their lives, and more able to contribute to community life. With time and a good database, economists and statisticians will be able to tease out the financial benefits of advancing healthcare IT.

Of course, money shouldn't be the only motivation. The deeper value of helping people stay healthy—so they can enjoy their lives, their families, their jobs, their futures—can't be measured in dollars. Neither can the most valuable return-on-investment of all: Saving lives.

The gap between what we know about preventing disease and what we're actually doing is vast. An estimated 80 percent of heart attacks and strokes, 80 percent of type 2 diabetes, and 40 percent of cancer could be prevented if Americans did just three things: stopped smoking, ate more healthy food, and exercised regularly.[7] Screening everyone eligible for a colon cancer check would save an estimated 75,000 lives each year.[8] Better preventive care could prevent 90 percent of diabetes complications,[9] 70 percent of asthma deaths,[10] and tens of thousands of life-altering hip fractures. By digitizing health, we can close this deadly gap. In fact, I believe real-time health care is the *only* way to bring the full force of evidence-based medicine and preventive care to every one of us.

This journey won't be simple or inexpensive. Industry must embrace information technology and all the promise offered by the capabilities, analytics, and data that will be unleashed once we fully automate health care. Once we understand that only a logged-in, real-time system can support great preventive care, we have an obligation to make this high ground our goal.

What will this new world look like? Moving to e-health won't be like stepping into a weird, George Jetson-style science-fiction future. It will be surprisingly familiar. Convenient. Immediate. And personal. We'll do away with the miles of medical folders now stashed behind thousands of receptionists' desks in doctors' offices across the country. We will put electronic records online and make them accessible to your doctors no matter where they are. You'll be able to log in to your personal health records at home to check on a lab test, schedule an appointment, or refill a prescription. No more waiting weeks for your medical records to travel across town, or enduring a long weekend waiting for your doctor to call Monday morning with test results. If you've ever tapped out an e-mail or answered a cell phone, you'll feel right at home in the world of e-health.

Saving Time, Money, Lives

Two case studies illustrate just how much health IT can improve care while cutting costs—and saving time—for everybody:

Faster, more accurate care is all digital. Children's Hospital of Pittsburgh went all-digital when it moved into its new building in the spring of 2009. Nearly 4,000 computers line the halls. Nurses swipe patients' wristbands with bar-code scanners to see when it's time for medication, and match the bar-coded dose to the prescription. In the intensive care unit, computer dashboards by patients' beds automatically graph vital signs and readings from monitors and lab tests—alerting nurses at a glance to drops and spikes that mean a patient might be having trouble. One result: Children's has seen medication errors drop 45 percent since it began automating health records in 2002. The system allows the hospital to track larger trends as well. When health IT head James Levin noticed too many doctors were ordering specially filtered blood for transfusions—typically needed by only a few patients—he asked for a review. At a price differential of $30 per bag, the hospital saved money without sacrificing good care.[11]

Less cost, no waiting? Just look to Denmark. Considered one of the world's most interconnected health systems, nearly every primary care physician in Denmark and almost half of hospitals use electronic medical records.

In windswept, rural Jutland, doctors at Thy-Mors Hospital review their patients' records on computer screens displaying a 3-D image of a human body. The doctor can rotate the image, and click to zoom in and get more information about a patient's back pains, heart disease, or arthritic knees—making it easy to get a full picture of their health.

Across Denmark, ambulances have access to medical records; crews can update files while they transport a patient to the emergency room. And millions of people use devices like electronic pulse readers that fit on their finger to do regular home check-ups. The info is sent to the doctor via a Bluetooth connection, and then discussed in a web chat with a doctor or a nurse. Electronic record-keeping saves the Danish health system an estimated $120 million a year, affords doctors nearly an extra hour every day to spend with patients, and makes medical appointments fast and easy for consumers—no one spends hours waiting for a 10-minute office visit.[12]

Portable Care: Health Information Exchanges

As health care deploys digital records, your own doctor will become more proactive in your health care. But what if you see more than one doctor, use prescription medicines, ever end up in the emergency room, or have ever switched from one practice to another? We all have—and that's why heath information exchanges (HIEs) must also emerge. As discussed in Chapter 3, when exchanges are in place, your health information can be shared among primary and specialty care physicians, hospitals, and anyone else focused on your health, as you permit. The EHR at Kaiser Permanente allowed Mary Gonzales's allergist to see that she needed a mammogram—and sign her up for one, on the spot. This demonstrates a sort of HIE among different Kaiser Permanente caregivers in an integrated system. But what if you had to see someone other than your regular doctor?

That's why HIE is so important. In and of themselves, electronic health records make it easier for your physicians to read their notes and your history. But they fall short of connecting various physicians in a virtual care team sharing information seamlessly on your behalf. This connectivity improves your chances for getting an accurate diagnosis, cuts your odds for undergoing duplicative medical tests, and speeds the time it takes to transfer medical records from hours, days, or weeks to a matter of seconds. Sharing your full history ensures that if you wind up in the emergency room while vacationing in Orlando, doctors will know about your drug allergies and your history of asthma even if your family doctor is thousands of miles away in Spokane. HIEs can help avoid dangerous drug interactions if you take medications prescribed by more than one doctor, and can keep track of your cumulative radiation exposure if you have a medical condition, such as kidney stones, that requires frequent CT scans.

HIEs are turning far-flung healthcare professionals into coordinated teams across the country. In Cleveland, Ohio, for example, nurses who staff walk-in mini-clinics in local drugstores can see the records of Cleveland Clinic patients. These retail health clinics are a fast, easy way to get relief for a sore throat or earache, but staff usually knows only what you tell them about your health history, leaving the door open for misinterpretations and for drug interactions. Teaming up in Cleveland also ensures that the mini-clinic visit automatically becomes part of a patient's permanent health record.[13]

On a smaller scale, mobile HIEs that use cell phones to transmit data are saving lives in dramatic ways. More and more heart cells die for every minute they are deprived of oxygen during a heart attack—never to be replaced. New "digital ambulances" are saving heart muscle in mountain-ous Santa Cruz County, California. Equipped with sophis-ticated cardiac monitors that can send vital data by cell phone directly to the emergency department of the receiv-ing hospital, this new system allows doctors to prepare more quickly for heart surgery once a heart-attack victim arrives. It's already showing results: Surgeons cleared a blocked artery in Alec Popovich's heart within 48 minutes of his arrival at the hospital—43 minutes faster than the hospi-tal's already fast average treatment time of 91 minutes.[14]

At Kaiser Permanente, HIEs are one reason heart attack death rates have fallen dramatically. The Clinical Pharmacy Cardiac Risk Service connects nurses, pharmacists, and doctors caring for 13,000 cardiac patients. Working together, this col-laboration has cut the risk of dying from a cardiac-related cause in the months after a heart attack by an amazing 88 percent.[15]

World-Class Care for Everyone: Care Registries

If this is all we do for health care, it would be a substantial improvement over the system as it is today. We could easily declare victory, take the savings created, and ride into the sunset.

But that would be a mistake. There's more we can do to take full advantage of the wondrous new tools IT is bringing to health care. With electronic medical records and HIEs up and running, we can add a level of care that customizes medicine's best practices for every patient. Called care registries or clinical decision support systems, these systems apply evidence-based guidelines to an individual's care. Essentially, they are very savvy safety nets—monitoring your vital signs, sleuthing for emerging risks, flashing reminders and alerts for your doctor, and comparing your treatment and outcomes against gold-standard care.

That's key. Right now in medicine, cutting-edge, research-based guidelines have been developed for preventing and treating hundreds of diseases. They work. Trouble is doctors don't always have the time or resources to learn and apply them. While care registries can't overcome barriers to healthcare delivery, they do give physicians the ability to know the trends, health risks, and opportunities across a given population, which is a breakthrough in itself.

Take type 2 diabetes. Experts estimate that fully 35 to 75 percent of the complications of this disease—horrific problems like blindness, kidney failure, heart attacks, and nerve and circulation problems that lead to amputations—could be avoided if doctors and patients followed established care guidelines. Most don't. As a result, 202,290 Americans with diabetes have end-stage kidney disease, 65,700 endure diabetes-related amputations of toes, feet, and legs each year, and 700,000 are at risk for blindness due to diabetes-related eye damage. People with diabetes are two to four times more likely to suffer a heart attack or stroke as someone without this blood-sugar problem.[16]

Care registries can turn this around. When researchers from the University of Minnesota, the Mayo Clinic, Wake Forest University, and other institutions tracked the benefits of a diabetes care registry installed in 24 doctors' practices across the nation, the results were nothing short of astonishing. In one year, foot exams increased 35 percent, eye exams rose 25 percent, and kidney-function testing increased 28 percent. Patients whose doctors used the new system were more likely to hit healthy blood sugar, cholesterol, and blood pressure targets. What did the system do? It analyzed patients' electronic medical records and churned out reminders for doctors. Results were summarized monthly so patients got close, continuing care.[17]

Care registries can also spot trouble early on. Consider asthma. Some 22 million Americans have this progressive lung problem. Despite great medications and established care routines, asthma accounts for 2 million emergency room visits, a half-million hospitalizations, and at least 4,000 deaths each year. Even mild asthma inflames airways in ways that do permanent damage, so early detection is key, especially in childhood.[18] To that end, an e-health system in Korea prevented a lot of potential damage by increasing the rates of early asthma diagnosis in kids by 20 percent.[19] And when the Emergency Department at Royal Prince Albert Hospital in New South Wales, Australia, installed an asthma care registry, the number of adults with asthma who left the ER with an asthma care plan for managing their condition increased seven-fold. That's important, because written action plans, with instructions for use of medications and advice on controlling personal asthma-attack triggers, can avert future emergencies and can even prevent deaths.[20]

Care registries have the potential to change how we treat some of our most vulnerable patients. A new digital registry for little hearts will, in a few years, help children born with life-threatening heart defects. Right now, these kids are treated with drugs and devices designed and tested not on tiny infants or toddlers but with adults in mind. Pediatric cardiologists have to go on instinct, off-the-cuff calculations, and reports from colleagues—rather than hard medical evidence—when treating some of medicine's smallest and sickest heart patients. Case in point: Doctors at Children's Hospital Boston say that of the 1,000 stents—metal tubes that keep blood vessels open—they've installed in children's hearts in recent years, none were used in ways approved or even evaluated by the FDA. The reason? There's no better fix. But now, a registry just started by the American College of Cardiology will gather and evaluate doctors' and patients' experiences with catheter-based heart procedures in children.

"We adopt things known to work in adult patients in pediatrics because we're sort of desperate," Gail Pearson, a pediatric cardiologist and medical officer for the Pediatric Heart Network, a clinical-trial cooperative of children's medical centers sponsored by the NIH's National Heart, Lung and Blood Institute told the *Wall Street Journal* in 2009. "We are trying to move more toward a paradigm where the norm would be if you're a child with complex clinical heart disease, your care would be guided by a research protocol" based on studies of children, she says.[21]

Future Health: Research and Predictive Care

It's safe to say preventive care is not a destination but a journey. As we bring these tools online and hone them, preventive care will continue to progress. As data is compiled and larger analyses are conducted, we will continuously improve outcomes on behalf of chronic patients and for people on the verge of disease, many of whom will never develop the disease at all.

We're reaching for that ultimate goal every time we use the stunning treasure trove of data stored in EHRs to conduct health research. I mentioned in Chapter 3 the Kaiser Permanente analysis of a database of 1.4 million members, which changed the course of medicine in 2004 when it found that the widely prescribed pain reliever Vioxx (rofecoxib) increased risk of heart attacks and sudden cardiac death. This drug and several other COX-2 inhibitors were responsibly pulled from the market, potentially saving tens of thousands of lives.[22]

Kaiser Permanente researchers are using electronic health databases to help us make smarter health decisions in daily life. For example: Is it safe for a breast cancer survivor to enjoy a glass of wine? A recent Kaiser Permanente study found that as few as three to four alcoholic drinks per week increased breast cancer recurrence by 30 percent.[23] Other research gives us license to enjoy life's pleasures with less guilt. In another recent Kaiser Permanente study, this time of the health records of 11,326 Canadians, researchers found that those carrying a *little* extra weight lived longer than those at a normal weight.[24] Maybe that slice of chocolate cake isn't so bad after all!

When your personal health history goes digital, you can opt to become part of this life-saving research effort. And research is vital. But one day, I believe e-health tools smarter than any we can imagine now will be able to analyze trends, spot emerging risks, discover which constellations of factors are the distant early warning signs of disease, and apply the knowledge directly to patient records in time to stop illness from ever happening.

This is the next frontier: predictive care. Thinkers, researchers, and IT developers are already diving in to develop tools that will accurately interpret the smallest shifts in your vital signs in order to keep you healthy. One day, these tools will teach themselves as they go along, essentially conducting their own research by searching for patterns in the health histories of thousands or even millions of people, then applying the knowledge to keep individuals healthy.

From Prevention to Prediction

Technology allows us to assess the potential for health and, often, to prevent illness. But will it save money? Yes. We will take redundancy and inefficiency out of the system. Healthier people are more productive on the job, more satisfied in their lives, and more able to contribute to community life.

Faster, more accurate care is all digital. It is integrated through HIEs. Teams of physicians, even those who practice at unrelated hospitals or in different cities, will be sharing information seamlessly on a patient's behalf. The health care of the future is customized. We are already using databases called care registries to apply evidence-based guidelines to an individual's care. They give physicians the ability to know the trends, health risks, and opportunities across a given population, which is a breakthrough in itself.

Predictive care is the next frontier. From databases of genetic profiles to digital tools that interpret the smallest shifts in your vital signs, we are developing the technology to anticipate illness and keep people healthy.

This is the power of real-time health care, uniting doctors and patients, healthcare payers, private industry, and government for the purpose of better, more personalized health care for all.

Notes

1. Kaiser Permanente, "Kaiser Permanente Members Talk about Our Vision in Action Today: Mary Gonzales's Story," http://xnet.kp.org/future/vision.html.

2. Jane Gross, "Why House Calls Save Money," *New York Times*, January 12, 2009, http://newoldage.blogs.nytimes.com/2009/01/12/why-house-calls-save-money/?scp=37&sq=percent22electronicpercent20medicalpercent20recordspercent22&st=cse.

3. "Central Maine Medical Center: Saving Lives," www.cmmc.org/about-saving-lives.

4. Sarah Kearns, "Hospital Uses EMRs to Avoid Drug Errors," *HealthLeaders Media*, August 31, 2009, www.healthleadersmedia.com/content/TEC-238222/Hospital-Uses-EMRs-to-Avoid-Drug-Errors.html.

5. Institute of Medicine of the National Academies Consensus Report, "Preventing Medication Errors," July 2006, www.iom.edu/~/media/Files/Report percent20Files/2006/Preventing-Medication-Errors-Quality-Chasm-Series/medicationerrorsnew.pdf.

6. D. P. Dunham, "Improving Medication Reconciliation in the 21st Century," *Current Drug Safety* 3, no. 3 (September 2008):227–229, www.ncbi.nlm.nih.gov/pubmed/18691006.

7. Susan J. Landers, "Chronic Diseases Poised for National Attention," *American Medical News*, June 4, 2007, www.ama-assn.org/amednews/2007/06/04/hlsc0604.htm.

8. Ibid.

9. American Diabetes Association, "Implications of the United Kingdom Prospective Diabetes Study," *Diabetes Care* 25, no. 1 (January 2002): s28–s32.

10. Matthew Mintz, "Asthma Update: Part I. Diagnosis, Monitoring, and Prevention of Disease Progression," *American Family Physician* 70, no. 5 (September 2004): 893–898, www.aafp.org/afp/2004/0901/p893.html.

11. Lauran Neergaard, "Paperless Health Care? A Hospital's Long Journey," The Associated Press, July 6, 2009, www.usatoday.com/news/health/2009-07-06-electronic-medical-records_N.htm.

12. Sindya Bhanoo, "Denmark Leads the Way in Digital Care," *New York Times*, January 12, 2010, www.nytimes.com/2010/01/12/health/12denmark.html.

13. Bernie Monegain, "Cleveland Clinic Partners with MinuteClinic, Links EMRs," *HealthcareIT News*, February 13, 2009, www.healthcare itnews.com/news/cleveland-clinic-partners-minuteclinic-links-emrs.

14. Liese Greensfelder, "Emergency Cardiac Monitoring Strategy Being Tested in Santa Cruz County Ambulances," University of California San Francisco News, December 10, 2003, www.ucsf.edu/news/2003/12/4715/emergency-cardiac-monitoring-strategy-being-tested-santa-cruz-county-amb.

15. Kaiser Per manente, "Electronic Health Records Help Cardiac Patients Remain Healthy," August 7, 2009, http://xnet.kp.org/news-center/pressreleases/co/2009/080709ehrcardiac.html, and Kari L. Olson, "Outcomes of Patients Discharged from Pharmacy-Managed Cardiovascular Disease Management," *American Journal of Managed Care* 15, no. 8 (2009): 497–503, www.ajmc.com/publications/issue/2009/2009-08-vol15-n8/AJMC_09aug_Olson_497to503/4.

16. American Diabetes Association, "Diabetes Statistics," www.diabetes.org/diabetes-basics/diabetes-statistics/.

17. Kevin A. Peterson, "Improving Diabetes Care in Practice. Findings from the TRANSLATE Trial," *Diabetes Care* 31, no. 12 (December 2008): 2238–2243, www.ncbi.nlm.nih.gov/pmc/articles/PMC2584171/.

18. Centers for Disease Control and Prevention, "Fastats: Asthma," www.cdc.gov/nchs/fastats/asthma.htm/.

19. K. H. Yoo, "The Impact of Electronic Medical Records on Timeliness of Diagnosis of Asthma," *The Journal of Asthma*, 44, no. 9 (November 2007): 753–758, www.ncbi.nlm.nih.gov/pubmed/17994406.

20. R. Kwok, "Improving Adherence to Asthma Clinical Guidelines and Discharge Documentation from Emergency Departments: Implementation of a Dynamic and Integrated Electronic Decision Support System," *Emergency Medicine Australasia* 21, no. 1 (February 2009):31–37, www.ncbi.nlm.nih.gov/pubmed/192543 10?itool=EntrezSystem2.PEntrez.Pubmed.Pubmed_ResultsPanel. Pubmed_RVDocSum&ordinalpos=14.

21. Ron Winslow, "Few Drugs or Devices to Treat Cardiovascular Disease Are Designed with Children in Mind," *Wall Street Journal*, August 12, 2009.

22. T. Craig Cheetham, "Myocardial Infarction and Its Association with the Use of Nonselective NSAIDs: A Nested Case-Control and Time-to-Event Analysis," *The Permanente Journal* 12, no. 1 (Winter 2008): 16–22, www.ncbi.nlm.nih.gov/pmc/articles/PMC3042333/.

23. Kaiser Permanente Press Release, "Alcohol Consumption May Increase Breast Cancer Recurrence Risk," December 10, 2009, www .dor.kaiser.org/external/news/press_releases/Alcohol_Consumption_ May_Increase_Breast_Cancer_Recurrence_Risk/.

24. Heather M. Orpana, "BMI and Mortality: Results from a National Longitudinal Study of Canadian Adults," *Obesity*, 18, no. 1 (2010): 214– 218, www.nature.com/oby/journal/v18/n1/full/oby2009191a.html.

Chapter 10

Connected System

Uniting Doctors, Patients, Payers, and Government

The age of real-time health care won't arrive tomorrow or next year: It's already here. Every day, more and more pieces of the nation's vast, wonderful, and revolutionary digital healthcare mosaic are falling into place:

- **More electronic health records (EHRs) in doctors' offices**. The percentage of non-hospital-based physicians with electronic health records systems doubled from 17 percent in 2008 to 34 percent in 2011.[1] Among them: America's Surgeon General Regina Benjamin, who switched her family practice on Alabama's Gulf Coast to a digital system in the aftermath of two hurricanes and a fire.[2]

- **Hospital EHRs skyrocket**. In just three years, the number of hospitals with EHRs has nearly tripled, from 13 percent in 2008 to 35 percent in 2011, according to the Office of the National Coordinator for Health Information Technology.[3] Government incentives ($5.6 billion by June 2012 to medical centers and physicians) are paying off. In the first big study of how EHRs affect hospital care, researchers from the University of Pennsylvania School of Nursing studied more than 16,000 nurses at 316 hospitals in four states. The nurses report fewer medical errors, better patient safety, and higher-quality care in digital hospitals.[4]

- **Medical labs are linking up**. Up to 80 percent of the information in your health record comes from lab test results.[5] Yet 7 in 100 "bad news" results aren't communicated to patients in a timely way.[6] With 8 billion (yes, *billion*) lab tests ordered annually in the United States,[7] that's a lot of missing data—and anxiety. Now, many of the 200,000 certified labs across America are taking steps to link electronically with doctors and hospitals. One great example: the state of Delaware, where 80 to 90 percent of lab results now flow through a single system to reach providers and medical centers electronically.[8] However, not all care systems are integrated, and even with EHRs, lab results can fall through the cracks before they reach patients. It will take more than technology; it will take leadership to solve this kind of healthcare delivery problem.

- **Interconnected systems from coast to coast**. Five American health systems—all of whom pioneered the adoption of electronic medical records (EMRs) for their own patients—recently forged a new alliance to exchange electronic health data securely among themselves. The five—Geisinger Health System (PA), Kaiser Permanente

(CA), Mayo Clinic (MN), Intermountain Healthcare (UT), and Group Health Cooperative (WA)—will pave the way for other health systems to share information. Ultimately, this consortium will be a model for systems that will let all hospitals and all healthcare providers exchange information. It's an important step toward our nation becoming a twenty-first century, information-enabled healthcare system.[9]

This revolution is moving at warp speed, yet we've got much farther to go. Even when most doctors and hospital systems are using electronic medical records systems, even when labs and specialists link up with them, and even when health information exchanges (HIEs) are up and running, the value these systems provide is limited if we have not fully connected *all patients* and *all caregivers* to *all relevant information in real time*.

For great results, we can't stop before we've got a system that's smart, networked, preventive, collaborative, and affordable. This chapter lays out a vision for a fully-connected, self-sustaining, health-focused future.

Connected Care: It's Personal

In 2012, more than two out of three Americans managed their bank accounts online. At least 80 percent of us shop online and many of us manage our credit cards online, too. So why not get the same 24/7 access to your health records? In one recent Deloitte survey, over 70 percent of Americans said they want their doctors to provide online access to medical records, test results, and appointment scheduling.[10] In the completely connected, real-time healthcare system of the future, you'll enjoy that convenience and much more. And much of it is available to Kaiser Permanente members today.

Here's a glimpse of a day in that connected world of your future health:

7:00 A.M. You log in to your personal health record from your mobile phone while your morning coffee brews. There's your latest cholesterol test—and a note from your doctor congratulating you on the weight loss, diet changes, and exercise program that are keeping your numbers within a healthy range. You notice that your blood pressure medications are ready for a refill, which you accomplish with a click.

7:20 A.M. You use your mobile phone to take a quick snapshot of the oatmeal, blueberries, and splash of low-fat milk you had for breakfast. The photos are transmitted to the weight-management plan in your online health record. It tallies the calories, fiber, fat, protein, and other nutrients automatically. You're off to a good start, even with the dab of brown sugar on your cereal.

Meanwhile, data from the three-mile walk you took with your dog at 6:00 A.M. has already been sent directly from your pedometer and from sensors woven into your exercise clothes to your online record. You take a peek. Wow! You burned 200 calories and kept your heart rate up for 30 minutes! Great job!

7:25 A.M. You fire off a quick e-mail to your doctor about your blood pressure. Your home monitor shows that your levels are staying within a healthy range. Could you cut back on your medications? You'd never do that on your own, of course. Your doctor can see your numbers because your blood pressure monitor also transmits info to your health record. That way, the two of you can collaborate on your care.

You're wondering what your next move is. Should you ramp up your weight loss efforts? Rein in blood pressure—raising sodium even further? You plan to check back at lunchtime for an answer . . . but your doctor's online this morning and before you know it, the two of you are Skyping—a quick, face-to-face meeting that didn't require a lengthy wait for the next appointment slot, another long wait in the waiting room, or taking time off from work. Good news! Your doctor says you can reduce the doses of your blood pressure medications—your doctor's office will e-mail the change to the pharmacy, pronto. She asks if you're keeping up with your stress-reduction routine, noting that last week you told her your mom's going into the hospital. "How's it going?" your doc asks. You're happy to report that 15 minutes of yoga at night is making you feel calm and relaxed—your wife and kids even notice the difference.

Before you sign off, your doctor's got some news. That new DNA check—the one that compares your personal genetic code with your health history and your family health history—shows that you're at increased risk for vision-robbing cataracts. Your doctor's already alerted your ophthalmologist, who will get back to you.

"And by the way," your doctor adds, "Congratulations on that fiftieth birthday. It's time for your colonoscopy. How about scheduling one?" You promise you'll do it today.

10:00 A.M. You check your health record during your morning break. There's a note from your eye doctor about that cataract risk. She tells you about an app for your mobile phone that can take high-resolution photos of your eyes. Could you download it and send her images of both eyes tonight? She'll have a special eyepiece delivered to your house today. And by the way, she noticed that you're due for your colonoscopy—could

177

you take a minute to schedule one? With a connected-care system, your entire care team's looking out for your whole health!

10:15 A.M. Okay, you really can't put this one off any longer. With a few clicks you've set up your colonoscopy. Waiting in your in-box is a link to a video about the procedure, plus directions for getting ready for the procedure. You know exactly what to expect.

Noon. Your oldest son needs to see an orthodontist. The dentist offered several recommendations. You spend a few minutes reading their performance data on their websites. You compare costs, length of treatment, adverse events, and can even see long-term results. One stands out from the crowd, so you send an e-mail to set up an appointment. Thank goodness you won't have to fill out all those basic forms when you get there. And your son won't need any duplicate X-rays. The information is all in his own electronic medical record, which everyone on his care team can access (with your permission, of course).

7:00 P.M. You stop by the hospital to visit your mother, who's just had knee replacement surgery. She arranged to have the procedure in a hospital near you instead of hundreds of miles away in her own community, so that she can recuperate at your place. Fortunately, your hospital's connected with healthcare systems across the nation—so her electronic medical record was accessible here. (That came in handy when she sprained her ankle during that Hawaiian vacation last summer, too.)

You breathe a sigh of relief, thinking about the hospital risks you *don't* have to worry about. Connected care means fewer in-hospital medication errors thanks to bar coding and lower risk for serious hospital-acquired infections. Mom uses insulin to control her diabetes; electronic health records even lower the risk for blood-sugar lows in the hospital that in the past meant longer stays, slower healing times, and even increased risk for dying.

Several nurses pop in to check on your mom during your visit. That's another perk courtesy of a connected system: Nurses with mobile devices linked to medical records can spend an additional 30 to 48 minutes caring for patients each shift.

Your mom's surgeon stops in for a brief check on his patient, who's doing well. He pulls out his mobile phone to check your mom's chart, and then explains that a new sterilization technique means he can even use his mobile in the OR to review patient info. He also mentioned that your mom's physical therapist uses a video "gaming" system to help people with new knees do their exercises the right way at home. Mom will exercise along with an interactive video—and results will be sent back to the therapist, who can analyze her progress and her needs. Sounds like something the grandkids will wish they could try!

8:00 P.M. **Time to test your eyes**. You unwrap the eyepiece that was waiting in a box on your doorstep when you got home. You follow the directions and in matter of minutes test your eyes, at home. You send your eye doctor a quick e-mail, alerting her that the test is done.

8:30 P.M. **You unroll your yoga mat and prop up your tablet computer to watch a yoga video selected from the health library connected to your medical record**. Your daughter wanders into the living room in her pajamas. Can she try it, too? You smile and give

her the mat—doing downward-facing dog on the car-
pet's a small price to pay for this kind of quality time
with your child. You're glad she's learning about the
importance of relaxation, too.

**10:00 P.M. The digital display along the edge of your
bathroom mirror flashes, reminding you to take
your blood-pressure medication—with the new
dosage**. You'd hate to miss a dose, but because you do
tend to forget pills, your doctor offered to set up this
can't-miss reminder system. Pretty amazing!

At Stake: Your Health *and* Your Money

Just a fantasy? In fact, every high-tech detail in this futuristic
scenario exists now or is in development. Health care of the
future will be completely patient-centered. And the benefits
go far beyond convenience. Technology-supported, real-time
health care is our best hope for meeting the critical health
challenges we face.

Thanks to an aging and increasingly overweight, inactive
population, the number of Americans with chronic health
conditions is rising sharply. That means more prescription
drugs, more doctor visits, more hospital stays, more lost work
time, more early deaths, and higher all-round healthcare costs.
In 2000, about 125 million Americans lived with one or more
chronic conditions such as diabetes, high blood pressure, heart
disease, and asthma.[11] But by the year 2030, that number will
increase 37 percent—to 171 million people.[12]

Just one of these, type 2 diabetes, could become the new
normal. The number of people with blood-sugar control
issues will increase from one in ten today to one in three by
2050, according to a 2010 report from the Centers for Disease

Control and Prevention published in the journal *Population Health Metrics*.[13] Diabetes raises odds for other serious, chronic threats—including vision loss, kidney failure, nerve damage, foot and leg amputations, and a two- to four-fold higher risk for heart attacks and strokes. Dramatic research proves that type 2 diabetes, the most common type of diabetes (type 1 diabetes is less common), can usually be prevented or delayed with something as simple as healthier choices, yet preventive health gets short shrift in today's system.

By the year 2030, at least half of the people coping with chronic health conditions will have more than one. Living with a constellation of chronic health challenges isn't easy or cheap. Chronic disease care uses 83 percent of our nation's healthcare dollars, according to the Robert Wood Johnson Foundation.[14] Compared with the lucky individual with no chronic health concerns, someone with five conditions gets 57 prescription-drug refills a year, goes to nine times more doctor visits, and is more likely to be hospitalized.[15]

Yet in our current disconnected, uncoordinated system, care for these people who need it most is forever falling between the cracks. More health care hasn't meant better health. They're at higher risk for unnecessary hospital stays because ongoing care is lacking. Odds are higher for dangerous drug reactions and interactions because they may be taking drugs prescribed by several different doctors. They're more likely to get duplicate tests because doctors and hospital systems aren't sharing information. And their care is compromised because they receive contradictory information from their disconnected providers.

The result: Poor health, despite a healthcare price tag three to fifteen times higher than it is for a patient with no chronic concerns. Connected systems are already saving health, saving lives, and saving money. A few inspiring examples:

- **A heart-health team that sees the big picture.** Coronary artery disease (CAD) affects 80 million Americans; those who've had one heart attack face one-in-five odds for dying within a decade. But in Colorado, Kaiser Permanente care teams enrolled 14,000 people with CAD in an electronic registry that coordinated every part of their care. **Results**: Healthy lifestyle steps, medication, tests, education, and quick follow-up of problems saved an estimated 135 lives and prevented 260 harrowing and costly emergency interventions. It's a win-win solution that's saved $21,900 per patient per year while vastly improving health. Eighty percent of participants brought their blood pressure down to healthier levels and 43 percent lowered their heart-threatening LDL cholesterol levels to a super-healthy 70 mg/dL or less.[16]

- **Back to basics for asthma care.** Great asthma care—the kind that keeps people out of the emergency room for wheezing and asthma attacks and lets them live the lives they want to live—depends on controlling airway inflammation in the lungs. But up to 7 in 10 kids and half of adults with asthma don't use steroid inhaler control medications regularly. Digital health catches and fixes that oversight, fast.[17] **Results:** EHRs helped family doctors in Spartanburg, South Carolina nearly double the number of patients with asthma who got their inhaled corticosteroid prescriptions filled.[18]

- **Attention to the details keeps people with diabetes healthier.** Every one-point rise in A1C results (a test of long-term blood sugar) boosts heart disease risk 14 percent for a person with diabetes.[19] High blood pressure and high cholesterol, common with this blood-sugar problem, further boost risk. Yet although 65 percent of all deaths in people with diabetes are the result of heart- and circulation-related problems,[20] 60 percent of people with diabetes said in one recent survey that they were unaware of the risk.[21] Protecting eyes and kidneys and sidestepping vulnerability to infections like the flu are also important concerns. Could electronic health records help patients and doctors stay on top of all of these details? **Results:** At several diabetes clinics in Cleveland, adoption of health IT means people with diabetes are one-third more likely to get great care, including eye exams, kidney-function checks, flu vaccines, and blood tests that measure long-term diabetes control. And patients were more likely to be at a healthy weight and have healthy blood pressure and blood sugar numbers.[22]

Proactive Care: It Really Works!

In Kaiser Permanente's Southern California region, proactive office encounters have contributed to a 30 percent increase in colon cancer screenings, an 11 percent increase in breast cancer screenings, a five percent increase in cervical cancer screening, and a 13 percent improvement in cholesterol control. How does it work? Because every provider on your care team sees your whole medical record, any provider you happen to be seeing will notice gaps in your care and encourage you to get the screenings you need. We project this will ultimately lead to 10,000 lives saved per decade.[23]

Nationally, the RAND Corporation estimates that widespread adoption of electronic medical records with alerts for colon cancer, breast cancer, and cervical cancer screenings and flu and pneumonia vaccines could save nearly 80,000 lives per year.[24]

Great connections also empower patients. Here at Kaiser Permanente, we analyzed the health outcomes of people who used our messaging system—a total of 556,000 secure patient-physician e-mail threads containing more than 630,000 messages were logged throughout the study. Patients initiated 85 percent of the threads: proof that this service really empowers people to better manage health. It worked. Their blood sugar, cholesterol, and blood pressure numbers improved by 2 to 6.5 percentage points.[25]

We're not alone. In New York City, a group of 309 family medicine practices adopted EHRs and found that patients' health improved on 8 of 10 preventive-care indicators. These included better blood pressure control, higher use of anticlotting medications, more flu vaccines and breast-cancer screenings, and more talks with patients about body weight and stop-smoking programs.[26]

Proactive care also helps with weight loss. In a study of 37 North Carolina family doctors, those whose EHR systems included a reminder about lifestyle interventions for obesity were 66 percent more likely to refer obese patients to healthy eating and exercise programs.[27]

It can also prevent broken bones and the disability this can cause. When doctors in the Pacific Northwest added reminders about brittle-bone screening to their digital toolbox, the number of women at high risk for bone fractures who received screening for osteoporosis increased significantly. The women, ages 50 to 85, had each already had at least one fracture: a warning sign for weakened bones. Just 5.6 percent of those doctors who didn't have computerized reminders received a bone mineral density test, compared to 51 percent who'd entered the digital age.[28]

What could be more proactive than using your own personal DNA data to guide your health care? The technology for mapping the human genome is now available to consumers. Right now it's expensive and results are difficult to interpret. But someday soon, the powerful health information locked inside your own DNA will be available to you as part of your electronic medical record. Even better, it will be paired with thoughtful analysis so you and your care team understand your risks and can choose the best steps for a healthy future. This could mean maintaining your fighting weight and regular exercise if you're a carrier of genes that boost diabetes risk, or earlier and more frequent colonoscopies or advanced breast imaging if you're at risk for cancers of the colon or breast.

Since 2007, researchers at Vanderbilt University and other institutions in the eMERGE (electronic MEdical Records and GEnomics) network have been comparing human genetic code with electronic medical records to find links between DNA, symptoms, and conditions. They've already turned up connections that could lead to personalized prescriptions for prevention and early detection of dementia, cataracts, peripheral artery disease, and type 2 diabetes—with more to come.[29]

Solving the Healthcare Spending Crisis

In 2010, healthcare spending in America topped $2.5 trillion. If we do nothing to control costs, the bill will nearly double—to $4.6 trillion—by the year 2020. I firmly believe that a fully connected system will go a long way toward resolving this crisis. Here's why.

First, a connected system has the power to eliminate vast amounts of waste. Experts including Donald M. Berwick, MD, MPP, FRCP, former administrator of the U.S. Centers for Medicare & Medicaid Services, estimate that a whopping 20 to 30 percent of healthcare costs are wasteful, delivering absolutely no health benefits to patients. Causes of waste include overtreatment, high administrative costs, fraud, and lack of care coordination that leads to duplicate tests, drug interactions, and patients who need more expensive treatments because they've fallen through the cracks in the system.

Cleaning up just one of these areas—duplicate and unnecessary tests (when was the last time you had to have a test repeated because a new doctor didn't have a copy of the results?)—could save the system $500 billion (yes, that's billion with a "b") a year!

Hospital stays account for about one-third of all health-care spending. Among Medicare patients, 18 percent of hospital stays are readmissions within 30 days of a first visit because something's gone wrong, a problem that costs about $15 billion a year.[30] The catch: 75 percent could be prevented if discharged patients received more attentive care in the days and weeks after leaving the hospital. And it can be done. At the Geisinger Health Plan in Pennsylvania, for example, a telehealth monitoring system for discharged hospital patients reduced the 30-day admission rate 44 percent.[31]

Ready to trim oversized administrative expenses? At Geisinger, information technology helped save $1.7 million over 5 years from reduced chart pulls; more than $600,000 from reduced printing and faxing; more than $500,000 per year from reduced nursing staff time through ePrescribing; and more than $1 million from reduced transcription costs. That's real money![32]

Getting There from Here: A Road Map

As I mentioned at the start of this chapter, Health IT is out of the starting gate and galloping. Google the term "health 2.0"—the catchphrase for patient-empowered, connected care—and you get nearly 600,000 hits. Search the phrase "electronic medical records" in PubMed, the National Library of Medicine's database of published research studies from around the world, and nearly 12,000 research papers turn up. With this much attention, is it safe to say that connected care is on its way—no help needed?

Not quite. It's going to take commitment and passion to fully connect our sprawling healthcare system. Stop short and you'll simply have really nifty replacements for manila-folder health records. They'll be electronic, but walled off in a "silo" at your doctor's office or hospital or in a local healthcare exchange. You—and all of us—will miss out on the data hiding inside: data that could help you get great care in a hospital far from home on vacation; data that could help researchers see new connections between genes and health risks, or learn something new about treating or preventing disease, or about treatment side effects.

It will take three factors to create real-time, completely connected health care: Innovative technology, passionate people, and a government that's willing to provide incentives rather than laying down onerous rules. Here's what I mean.

Factor #1: Rapid Growth of Investments in Innovative Technology

In this book we explored the explosion of innovation around electronic medical records and connectivity. From wearable health sensors to the Blue Button that lets consumers download relevant data in a flash, from the capability to analyze enormous data sets to telemonitoring in your home, new developments number in the thousands and are growing exponentially.

That's exactly what needs to happen. It's the right way to go: It's the American way and it creates flexible, nimble, adaptable systems that meet real and changing healthcare and IT needs. Innovators have brought us over 1,000 different electronic medical record systems—from pricey models with all the bells and whistles to simple systems that store a doctor's patient records on the Cloud for less than $20 per month, with no need to buy new equipment or hire a computer guru for weeks on end.

Technology that makes health care easier, more convenient, and more personal for everyone who encounters it will be transformative—whether it's a program that translates medical terms into everyday language, a scheduling app that makes getting in to see your doctor a breeze, or a ratings tool that gives you a detailed picture of your doctor's performance. The practice of medicine, and the experience of medicine, will become more intimate, bringing it back into the privacy and convenience of our homes.

And innovation will drive down costs. Yes, in some nations government has led the way in controlling the costs of health care, but that's not our way. Innovators who find real solutions, I believe, will also make a connected system affordable for us and profitable for them: the kind of win–win that really works.

Factor #2: People with Passion, Patience, Determination

You can have all the money, all the technology, and all the incentives and rules in the world, but it takes commitment to achieve great health IT. As David Blumenthal, MD, MPP, past national coordinator of the Office of the National Coordinator for Health Information Technology wrote recently, "The exchange of information is going to be one of the most ambitious healthcare social projects that we ever undertake. The mapping of the human genome will look simple in comparison. The reason is that it's a human-ware problem, not a software problem . . . *Health informa-tion exchange is a team sport.* Using a football analogy, you can be Tom Brady or Peyton Manning, but if you don't have a receiver down the field, you might as well not show up."

Dr. Blumenthal's comments appear in the 2012 Robert Wood Johnson Foundation report "Health Information Technology in the United States: Driving toward Delivery System Change." He says our industry has to overcome the "the Toyota/BMW effect"—recognizing that asking competing hospitals in a community, or competing physician's practices, to send their own clients' data to their competitors' computer systems goes against basic business instincts.[33]

Seeing the bigger benefits—the health benefits for patients—can overcome distrust and disinterest. It also helps to remember that cost savings will flow back to you. And that being connected will soon be part of the definition of a great hospital, a terrific doctor. Patients are coming to expect it. Making decisions to cross old boundaries and share data is just good business.

Enthusiasm and determination count inside an organization, too. Back in 2005, French researchers reviewed the adoption of electronic medical records at the University Hospital of Rennes. Motivation ranked among the key factors driving the success of the project. It takes health IT champions who can explain the benefits over and over again, while providing plenty of training and support, who make things happen—people who "embrace change, contribute enthusiastically, and have the respect of their peers."[34]

It takes real cultural change to connect within a practice or a hospital—and between systems. Done right, it can make the system stronger.

Factor #3: Government Incentives, Not Heavy Mandates

Rules and incentives have worked to spur wider adoption of digital records and connected systems; now it's time for government to encourage innovation. State and federal government shouldn't mandate everything. That's not our culture and it's not what works best.

Yes, doctors and hospitals have benefited from government grants to set up digital records systems.

But where government may really make a big contribution is with moves like the Investing in Innovation initiatives (i2) launched by the Office of the National Coordinator for Health Information Technology. The latest initiative asks tech innovators to create an app that will allow eye doctors to download information and images from a variety of eye tests—all typically stored in databases and file formats with little connectivity to digital records—easily into patient records. The prize: $100,000. But the rewards will go far beyond the check when an innovative solution breaks down barriers so that health care can be delivered, with ease, in the blink of an eye.[35, 36]

Conclusion

If you take away only one thing from this book, I hope it is the conviction that transforming health care through the use of health IT is essential to building the healthcare system we need; a system that is:

- **Connected,** beginning with EMRs that are part of an HIE that follows a patient throughout her life.
- **Consistent,** so it can be shared through HIEs and added to care registries and databases where it can advance our

understanding of disease, treatment, and prevention, leading to better health for all.

- **Mobile,** allowing patients, physicians, and other caregivers to meet, converse, and exchange information of all
sorts from anywhere.

- **Personal,** achieved by giving individuals more transpar-
ent and secure access to their own data (including their
own genetic makeup) and by tapping into the masses of
data that will be generated by the technologies described
in this book, and others that have yet to be dreamed of.

No one can deny that the stakes are high. The amount
spent on health care in the United States is unsustainable.
The United States spends the highest percentage of its GDP
on health care in the world (18 percent in 2010; 19 percent
projected in 2020).[37] Yet, we do not see the kind of health
outcomes that one would expect that level of expenditure
to buy. Indeed, most doctors and healthcare providers in this
country are paid to treat illness, order tests, and deliver treatment, not to ensure health. Too many hospitals put an empty
bed on the debit side of the ledger. Instead, we should see
empty hospital beds as a credit to the quality of preventive
care being delivered.

But the rewards we stand to gain are even higher. Some
rewards are financial; reducing our overall healthcare expenditures would strengthen our economy overall and ease the
financial burden on individuals and families. Private sector
companies, large and small, that participate in the healthcare
IT transformation will deserve to prosper from their con-
tributions. Even healthcare plans and payers stand to reap
financial benefits for the effort they put into change. Better
health outcomes also have financial implications: People will

be more productive on the job and have more discretionary income without big pharmacy bills to pay each month.

And of course, the biggest rewards are intangible: a better start in life for babies born to women who get good prenatal care; active, happy children who never know the clutching terror of an asthma attack; the peace of mind of women who don't have to fear breast cancer and men relieved of the specter of prostate cancer; more years to spend with the grandkids. Not to mention the satisfaction of a doctor or nurse over a job well done, another patient well cared for.

We hold the key to all of this in our hands: information leveraged through technology. I hope you will be motivated to join me in using that key to open the door and step into the transformed future of health care.

Notes

1. Chun-Ju Hsiao, "Electronic Health Record Systems and Intent to Apply for Meaningful Use Incentives among Office-Based Physician Practices: United States, 2001–2011," National Center for Health Statistics Data Brief Number 79, November 2011, www.cdc.gov/nchs/data/databriefs/db79.htm.

2. Regina Benjamin, "Finding My Way to Electronic Health Records," *New England Journal of Medicine* 363 (2010): 505–506, www.nejm.org/doi/full/10.1056/NEJMp1007785.

3. Dustin Charles, "Electronic Health Record Systems and Intent to Attest to Meaningful Use among Non-Federal Acute Care Hospitals in the United States: 2008–2011," ONC Data Brief no. 1, February 2012, www.healthit.gov/media/pdf/ONC_Data_Brief_AHA_2011.pdf.

4. Ann Kutney-Lee, "The Effect of Hospital Electronic Health Record Adoption on Nurse-Assessed Quality of Care and Patient Safety," *Journal of Nursing Administration* 41 (November 2011): 466–472, www.ncbi.nlm.nih.gov/pubmed/22033316.

5. ONC State HIE Cooperative Agreement Technical Assistance Program, "Laboratory Interoperability: Requirements, Challenges, Strategies," June 20, 2011, ppt. see slide 3.

6. AHRQ, Frequency of failure to inform patients of clinically significant outpatient test results. Casalino LP, Dunham D, Chin MH. 2009 http://psnet.ahrq.gov/resource.aspx?resourceID=10345.

7. Edward R. Pinckney, "The Accuracy and Significance of Medical Testing," *Archives of Internal Medicine* 143, no. 3 (1983): 512–514, http://archinte.jamanetwork.com/article.aspx?articleid=602917.

8. ONC State HIE Cooperative Agreement Technical Assistance Program, "Laboratory Interoperability: Requirements, Challenges, Strategies," June 20, 2011, ppt. see slides 12, 13.

9. Kaiser Permanente press release, "Five Leading Health Systems Create New Care Connectivity Consortium." April 6, 2011. http://xnet .kp.org/newscenter/pressreleases/nat/2011/040611interoperability.html

10. Anna-Lisa Silvestre, "If You Build It, Will They Come? The Kaiser Permanente Model of Online Health Care," *Health Affairs* 28, no. 2, http://content.healthaffairs.org/content/28/2/334.abstract.

11. Robert Wood Johnson Foundation, "Chronic Conditions: Making the Case for Ongoing Care," December 2002, www.rwjf.org/files/ research/chronicbook2002.pdf.

12. Robert Wood Johnson Foundation, "Improving Chronic Illness Care: An RWJF National Program," September 2011, www.rwjf .org/files/research/CDM.final.pdf.

13. James P. Boyle, "Projection of the Year 2050 Burden of Diabetes in the U.S. Adult Population: Dynamic Modeling of Incidence, Mortality, and Prediabetes Prevalence," *Population Health Metrics* 8, no. 29 (2010), www.pophealthmetrics.com/content/8/1/29/.

14. Robert Wood Johnson Foundation, "Chronic Conditions."

15. Gerard Anderson, "Chronic Conditions: Making the Case for Ongoing Care," Johns Hopkins Bloomberg School of Public Health, November 2007, 34, 35.

16. Kaiser Permanente SmartBook Highlight, KP HealthConnect and KP.org Value Realization, November 2010. http://crdc-apps15 .kp.org:8080/business/kpit/kphealthconnect/smartbook.nsf/2d5e5

35f7682ef2b882572b8007cf3ea/3b65250a145a839f8825790b00669 fa0?OpenDocument&Highlight=0,21,900.

17. Yitzhak Katz, "Non-Adherence, Non-Compliance or Non-Concordance in Asthma: Patients Not Following the Medical Regimen," *IMAJ* 9 (2007): 389–390, www.ima.org.il/imaj/ ar07may-13.pdf.

18. A. M. Davis, "Using the Electronic Medical Record to Improve Asthma Severity Documentation and Treatment among Family Medicine Residents," *Family Medicine* 42 (May 2010): 334–337, www.ncbi.nlm.nih.gov/pubmed/20455109.

19. Elizabeth Selvin, "Meta-Analysis: Glycosylated Hemoglobin and Cardiovascular Disease in Diabetes Mellitus," *Archives of Internal Medicine* 141, no. 6 (September 21, 2004): 421–431, www.ncbi.nlm .nih.gov/pubmed/15381515.

20. American Heart Association, "Cardiovascular Disease & Diabetes," www.heart.org/HEARTORG/Conditions/Diabetes/WhyDiabetes Matters/Cardiovascular-Disease-Diabetes_UCM_313865_Article.jsp.

21. WebMD, "Most Diabetics Unaware of Heart Risk," http://diabetes .webmd.com/news/20020220/most-diabetics-unaware-of-heart-risk.

22. Randall D. Cebul, "Electronic Health Records and Quality of Diabetes Care," *New England Journal of Medicine* 365 (2011): 825–833, www.nejm.org/doi/pdf/10.1056/NEJMsa1102519.

23. Kaiser Permanente, Case Study, "Proactive Office Encounter: Better Care through Coordinated Teams and Health Information Technology," http://xnet.kp.org/reform/docs/case_studies/case_ study_proactive_officer.pdf.

24. RAND Corporation, "Health Information Technology: Can HIT Lower Costs and Improve Quality?" www.rand.org/pubs/research_ briefs/RB9136/index1.html.

25. Yi Yvonne Zhou, "Improved Quality at Kaiser Permanente through E-Mail between Physicians and Patients," *Health Affairs* 29, no. 7 (July 2010): 1370–1375, http://content.healthaffairs.org/content /29/7/1370.abstract.

26. Samantha F. De Leon, "Tracking the Delivery of Prevention-Oriented Care among Primary Care Providers Who Have Adopted Electronic Health Records," *Journal of the American Medical Informatics*

Association 18, suppl. 1 (December 2011), http://jamia.bmj.com/content/early/2011/08/18/amiajnl-2011-000219.abstract.

27. S. P. Schriefer, "Effect of a Computerized Body Mass Index Prompt on Diagnosis and Treatment of Adult Obesity," *Family Medicine* 41, no. 7 (July–Aug 2009): 502–507, www.ncbi.nlm.nih.gov/pubmed/19582636.

28. A. Feldstein, "Electronic Medical Record Reminder Improves Osteoporosis Management after a Fracture: A Randomized, Controlled Trial," *Journal of the American Geriatric Society* 54, no. 3 (March 2006): 450–457, www.ncbi.nlm.nih.gov/pubmed/16551312.

29. Vanderbilt University, "The eMERGE (Electronic MEdical Records and GEnomics) Network," https://www.mc.vanderbilt.edu/victr/dcc/projects/acc/index.php/Main_Page.

30. MedPac Report to Congress, "Promoting Greater Efficiency in Medicare, Chapter 5: Payment Policy for Inpatient Readmissions," June 2007, www.medpac.gov/chapters/Jun07_Ch05.pdf.

31. Chris Anderson, "Geisinger Telehealth Program Helps Reduce Hospital Readmissions," *Healthcare Information and Management Systems Society News*, March 1, 2012, www.mhimss.org/news/geisinger-telehealth-program-helps-reduce-hospital-readmissions.

32. Bernie Monegain, Top CEOs Offer Checklist for Better Healthcare," *Healthcare IT News*, June 11, 2012, www.healthcareitnews.com/news/top-ceos-offer-checklist-better-healthcare.

33. Robert Wood Johnson Foundation, "Health Information Technology in the United States: Driving Toward Delivery System Change," 2012, www.google.com/url?sa=t&rct=j&q=&esrc=s&source=web&cd=1&ved=0CGgQFjAA&url=http%3A%2F%2Fwww.rwjf.org%2Fqualityequality%2Fproduct.jsp%3Fid%3D74262&ei=KCcMUIusG4fx0gG6v_z9Aw&usg=AFQjCNFAoO5D-c6qfM1n6u85uOory0Etig.

34. José Luis Sánchez, "Key Success Factors in Implementing Electronic Medical Records in University Hospital of Rennes," Europhamili/Aesculapius Professional Study, ENSP Rennes, France, 2005, www.google.com/url?sa=t&rct=j&q=&esrc=s&source=web&cd=1&ved=0CGgQFjAA&url=http%3A%2F%2Fciteseerx.ist.psu.edu-%2Fviewdoc%2Fdownload%3Fdoi%3D10.1.1.138.7389%26rep%3

Drep1%26type%3Dpdf&ei=YycMUI7YAqrn0QHT6-j1Aw&usg=
AFQjCNE3qshSAtcc8-OqyRu8vbnA4GwjWQ.

35. U.S. Department of Health and Human Services, "HHS and the Office
of the National Coordinator for Health Information Technology
Introduce New Investing in Innovations (i2) Initiative," June 8, 2011,
www.hhs.gov/news/press/2011pres/06/20110608a.html.

36. U.S. Department of Health and Human Services, "ONC
Launches New i2 Ocular Imaging Challenge," May 18, 2012,
http://www.healthit.gov/buzz-blog/health-innovation/
i2-ocular-imaging-developer-contest/.

37. Centers for Medicare & Medicaid Services, Office of the Actuary.
"National Health Expenditures and Selected Economic Indicators,
Levels and Annual Percent Change: Calendar Years 2006-2021"
January 2012. www.cms.gov/Research-Statistics-Data-and-Systems/
Statistics-Trends-and-Reports/NationalHealthExpendData/
Downloads/Proj2011PDF.pdf.

About the Author

PHILIP FASANO is a nationally recognized leader in information technology. As executive vice president and chief information officer of Kaiser Permanente, the nation's largest not-for-profit health plan and health care provider, he leads its efforts to harness technology to deliver real-time, personalized health care to its nine million members.

Fasano also served in information technology leadership roles in some of the nation's top finance companies, including Capital One Financial Group, JP Morgan, and Deutsche Financial Services, a division of Deutsche Bank. He earned an MBA from Long Island University and a BS in Computer Science from the New York Institute of Technology. He lives in Alamo, California and has deep roots in Northern Virginia.

Index

Index

Index

Index